Watch Your Spirit Soar

Astral projection, or out-of-body travel, is a completely natural experience. You've probably already astral traveled thousands of times in your sleep, you just don't remember it when you wake up. Now you can learn how to leave your body at will, be fully conscious of the experience, and remember it when you return.

By the time you have finished the exercises in this book you will be able to watch your spirit soar as you:

- Instantly visit any place in the world that you desire
- Transport yourself back and forward through time
- Speak freely with people from any time and any culture
- Lose any fear of death
- Find love on the astral plane
- Keep an eye on loved ones and friends
- Astral travel in your sleep
- Practice remote viewing without leaving your body
- Use numerology to find which days will be easier for you to astral project
- Take an astral trip with another person
- Visit the deceased and even carry on a relationship with them

About the Author

Richard Webster was born in Auckland, New Zealand in 1946. New Zealand is still his home, though he travels widely every year lecturing and conducting workshops on psychic subjects around the world. He is a prolific author and also writes monthly columns for two magazines. Richard began his working life in publishing, and became in turn a bookstore proprietor, pianist, stage hypnotist, palmist, ghostwriter, and magician before becoming a professional teacher and writer on psychic topics.

ASTRAL TRAVEL
for BEGINNERS

Richard Webster

2002
Llewellyn Publications
St. Paul, Minnesota 55164-0383, U.S.A.

FIRST EDITION
Fourth Printing, 2002

Cover design: Tom Grewe
Interior Illustrations: Jeannie Ferguson
Editing and typesetting: Marguerite Krause
Book design: Astrid Sandell

Library of Congress Cataloging-in-Publication Data
Webster, Richard, 1946-
   Astral travel for beginners / Richard Webster. — 1st ed.
     p.   cm.
   Includes bibliographical references and index.
   ISBN 1-56718-796-X (pbk.)
   1. Astral projection.   I. Title.
   BF1389.A7W43   1998
   133.9'5—dc21   98-13689
                                             CIP

Llewellyn Worldwide does not participate in, endorse, or have any authority or responsibility concerning private business transactions between our authors and the public.

All mail addressed to the author is forwarded but the publisher cannot, unless specifically instructed by the author, give out an address or phone number.

Llewellyn Publications
A Division of Llewellyn Worldwide, Ltd.
P.O. Box 64383, Dept. 796-X
St. Paul, MN 55164-0383, U.S.A.
www.llewellyn.com

Printed in the United States of America.

Dedication

For Docc, Caroline, and Peyton
Three special friends

Other Books by Richard Webster

101 Feng Shui Tips for the Home
Spirit Guides and Angel Guardians
Aura Reading for Beginners
Dowsing for Beginners
Feng Shui for Beginners
Omens, Oghams & Oracles
Revealing Hands
Seven Secrets to Success
Numerology Magic (formerly *Talisman Magic)*
Chinese Numerology
Feng Shui for Apartment Living
Feng Shui for the Workplace
Feng Shui for Love & Romance
Feng Shui in the Garden
Feng Shui for Success & Happiness
Palm Reading for Beginners
The Complete Book of Palmistry
    (formerly *Revealing Hands)*
Soul Mates
Write Your Own Magic
Pendulum Magic for Beginners
Practical Guide to Past-Life Memories

Contents

Introduction   ix

Chapter One   1
Astral Travel Requirements

Chapter Two   13
A Few Definitions

Chapter Three   23
Involuntary Astral Travel

Chapter Four   45
Getting Started

Chapter Five   57
The Astral World

Chapter Six   71
Your First Astral Travel

Chapter Seven   81
Advanced Astral Travel

Chapter Eight   93
Exploring Different Worlds

Chapter Nine   101
Other Methods of Astral Traveling

Chapter Ten   135
Astral Traveling in Your Sleep

Chapter Eleven   149
Traveling in Pairs

Chapter Twelve   165
Group Astral Travel

Chapter Thirteen   179
   Experiments in Remote Viewing

Chapter Fourteen   187
   Numerology and Astral Travel

Chapter Fifteen   195
   Conclusion

Appendix   197

Notes   203

Glossary   213

Suggested Reading   219

Index   223

Introduction

ASTRAL TRAVEL HAS FASCINATED PEOPLE FROM THE beginning of time. How was it that some people were able to transcend time and space, leave their physical bodies, and go wherever they wished? Was this talent available to just a few people or could anyone learn to do it? Naturally, the shamans who astral traveled to find glimpses of the future or answers to questions had a vested interest in keeping their simple techniques a secret. Their power would vanish if everyone was able to astral travel.

However, throughout history a few people have found themselves spontaneously astral traveling. In most cases, this was a pleasant experience, but some found it terrifying, and the stories of their experiences have made the very idea of astral traveling frightening for many.

My first astral travel was completely spontaneous, but fortunately was not frightening. I was fifteen years old at the time. One afternoon I was trying to find some information in the school library before going home. I knew that I was in danger of missing the train, but was trying to find some important information for my homework before leaving. All of a sudden, I found myself at the railway station with the other students. I seemed to be my normal self in every way, except that I was aware that I was out of my physical body. There was the usual horseplay going on and I decided to see if the others were aware of my presence. I gave a friend a playful slap on the back and found my hand went right through him. Neither he nor anyone else noticed anything; therefore, I knew that the others could not see me. I yelled a greeting to my friend, but received no response. I suddenly realized that I had left my school bag behind. As soon as I became aware of this I found myself back in the school library. I hastily packed my bag and ran for the train, but missed it.

I spent forty-five minutes waiting for the next train, which gave me plenty of time to think about the experience. I had previously read several books on astral travel, particularly the works of Sylvan Muldoon, so I was not particularly surprised that it had happened. However, although I had read about astral travel, I had never tried to do it. This experience provided the necessary impetus and desire to learn how to astral travel whenever I wished.

Thinking back on the experience, I realize now that all the right conditions were there for an out-of-body experience. I was desperately trying to find information in the school library and was in a hurry because I did not want to miss the train. Both of these factors created stress. I had also read about the subject and wanted to astral travel, so the desire to do it was there as well. A stressful situation, combined with desire, is an ideal scenario for an involuntary astral travel.

Many people think that leaving the physical body is dangerous. In fact, astral traveling is much safer than driving down the road in your car. In this book we will approach the subject in the safest way possible. For many years I guided students in my psychic development classes through their first astral travels. None of them had any problems, and all found their lives enhanced by this useful skill.

What is astral travel? Astral travel simply means leaving your physical body behind, going wherever you want to go, and then returning to the body. A more accurate name is "Out-of-Body Experience," commonly known as OBE or OOBE for short.

Since the dawn of history, there have been reports of people who have been able to astral travel. Descriptions of prehistoric astral travels have come from Egypt, India, China, and Tibet. In Tibet, people who astral traveled were called *delogs*, which means "those who return from the Beyond."[1]

The ancient Egyptians believed in Ka (the astral double) and Ba (the soul or spirit), and believed that both were able to leave the body whenever they wished. In

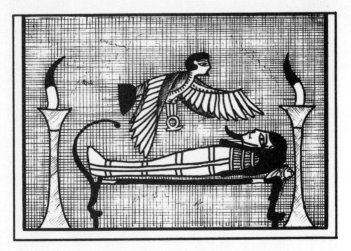

FIGURE 1. *The Egyptian Ka.*

his introduction to the *Egyptian Book of the Dead*, E. A. Wallis Budge wrote that the ancient Egyptians saw the Ka as being an abstract body that looked like and possessed the qualities of the person it belonged to. However, it was also independent and free to move away from the physical body whenever it wished.

Plato believed that the life we lead inside our physical bodies was a pale imitation of what the spirit would see once it was free of the physical. Aristotle believed that the spirit could leave the body and communicate with the spirits. The Greeks also believed that we possess a second, subtle body.

In the Bible there is a reference to astral travel when "the spirit of the Lord caught away Philip" after a baptism and he "was found at Azotus."[2]

In the *Epistle to the Corinthians*, Paul writes: "I knew a man in Christ above fourteen years ago . . . caught up to the third heaven . . . into paradise, and heard unspeakable words, which is not lawful for a man to utter."[3]

In the Druidic tradition, there is an old story about Mog Ruith, a druid from West Munster who was able to fly over the heads of an opposing army and bring back details of the enemy while wearing a bird costume.[4] This is obviously an account of astral travel.

In 1808, Herr Wesermann, a German businessman, found he was able to astral travel and "appear" in the dreams of his friends. He conducted a series of experiments and in four of them his friends saw what he wanted them to see in their dreams.

The fifth experiment was highly intriguing. Lieutenant N. was supposed to have a dream at 11:00 P.M. and see a lady who had been dead for five years. As it happened, Lieutenant N. stayed up late that night, discussing the campaign against the French with a friend. At 11:00 P.M. the door opened, and in walked the lady, dressed in white with a black kerchief and bare head. She nodded at the lieutenant's friend three times and then nodded in his direction. Smiling slightly, she turned around and went back out the door. The two men were stunned for a few moments, but then raced out the door after her. The woman had disappeared, and the sentinel at the entrance swore that he had seen nothing.[5]

The first scientific experiments into astral travel were performed at the end of the nineteenth century by the French scientist Hector Durville. He utilized a subject who claimed to be able to leave his body whenever he wished. While he was out of his body, this man managed to make rapping sounds on a table at the far end of the room, create a fogging effect on photographic plates, and cause calcium sulphide screens to become brighter.

Madame Blavatsky, or H.P.B. as she is known to Theosophists, founded the Theosophical Society in New York in 1875. She claimed to have spent some forty years traveling in the East and learning from the masters there. Her society put forward the idea that we are not simply the product of our physical bodies, but are made up of at least seven bodies, rather like a series of garments. The Theosophical Society had an enormous influence in promoting astral travel, as well as many other aspects of Eastern philosophy.

The subject of astral travel gained enormous popularity during the twentieth century. While World War I was laying waste to most of Europe, two men were quietly experimenting with astral projection. The first of these was Hugh Callaway, an engineer and Theosophist, whose book, *Astral Projection*, is still one of the most readable books on the subject. His book, published under the pseudonym "Oliver Fox," appeared shortly before World War II and is based largely on two lengthy articles he wrote for the *Occult Review* in 1920. The second man lived across the English Channel. He was the French mystic Marcel Louis Forhan, who used the pseudonym "Yram" when he wrote *Le Médecin de l'Ame*, which was published in English as *Practical Astral Projection*.

A decade later, Sylvan Muldoon was experimenting with astral travel in the United States. His first book, *The Projection of the Astral Body*, was written with Hereward Carrington and appeared in 1929. Unlike Oliver Fox and Yram, who appeared to believe that only certain people could astral travel, Sylvan Muldoon believed that anyone could do it, and collected accounts of people who had spontaneously left their bodies and safely returned.

In the 1960s, Sylvan Muldoon's work was taken several steps further by Dr. Robert Crookall, a retired geologist, who collected numerous accounts of astral travels and carefully analyzed and evaluated them. In the space of ten years he collected and wrote about 750 different cases. His first book on the subject, *The Study and Practice of Astral Projection*, was published in 1960.

Dr. Crookall carefully evaluated each case, looking for common factors that would help him understand the phenomenon better. After much study, he found that there were six characteristics that applied to everyone he assessed:

1. The subjects feel that they are leaving their bodies out of the top of their heads.

2. The subjects black out for a second at the exact instant their astral and physical bodies separate.

3. The subjects' astral bodies float above the physical bodies for a while before moving away.

4. The astral bodies float again over the physical bodies before returning.

5. The subjects black out again momentarily as their astral body returns.

6. When the astral body returns too quickly, the subjects' bodies are buffeted and jolted.

Very little serious scientific exploration was done on out-of-body experiences before Dr. Crookall took an interest. However, since his studies became available, a large number of scientists have conducted surveys and found that many more people had experienced out-of-body experiences than had previously been thought.

Since Dr. Crookall's time, Celia Green of the Institute of Psychophysical Research has collected many more cases of out-of-body experiences. Her survey is the most thorough so far, and included people from all walks of society, located through advertisements in the press.[6]

Although scientists found that their results varied from country to country, it appears that some twenty percent of the world's population will experience an out-of-body experience at some time during their lives.[7] University students seem to be more likely to leave their bodies than other people. Celia Green found that thirty-four percent of the Oxford undergraduates in her 1968 study had left their bodies at least once. A larger survey, taken in 1975, revealed that twenty-five percent of the students surveyed had had an out-of-body experience, compared to fourteen percent among the general population. To confuse things even further, when an American magazine asked its readers if they had astral traveled, 700 of the 1,500 replies, or 46.6 percent, claimed that they had.[8]

A survey conducted by Dr. Stewart Twemlow of the Topeka VA Medical Center was presented at the annual convention of the American Psychiatric Association in 1980. He found that eighty-five percent of the people who had astral traveled enjoyed the experience, and more than half of them described it as "joyful." "Fully forty-three percent of the subjects considered it to be the greatest thing that had ever happened to them," Dr. Twemlow reported.[9] No wonder most of them wanted to astral travel again. The singer Kate Bush once described the experience as being like a "kite" that is loosely tethered to the body and able to float freely.[10] My students all agreed with her excellent description.

Today, many parapsychologists are exploring remote viewing, which is a form of astral travel. In remote viewing, the person being tested is asked to describe locations, objects, and activities that are going on in a particular place, which may be thousands of miles away.

The increasing interest that scientists are showing is very encouraging. Dr. Eugene E. Bernard, professor of psychology at North Carolina State University, said, "It is improbable that so many people who are apparently psychologically healthy are having hallucinations. There is still much we don't know about the mind and its abilities. I don't know how long it will take, but I believe the astral projection theory can be proved and controlled."[11]

There have also been countless personal accounts of leaving the body. One well-known example was first recorded as Case Fourteen in Edmund Gurney's fascinating book *Phantasms of the Living*, which recounts 702 psychic experiences. In November 1881, Mr. S. H. Beard successfully astral traveled to his fiancée's bedroom. He wrote, "On a certain Sunday evening in November, 1881, having been reading of the great power which the human will is capable of exercising, I determined with the whole force of my being, that I would be present in spirit in the front bedroom on the second floor of a house situated at 22 Hogarth Road, Kensington." This room was shared by his fiancée, Miss L. S. Verity and her eleven-year-old sister.

Mr. Beard lived about three miles away from Miss Verity and did not tell her what he was planning to do. When he saw her on the following Thursday, she immediately told him how terrified she had been on the previous Sunday evening because she had seen him standing beside her bed. She had screamed when he moved towards her. These screams woke up her sister, who also saw the apparition.

Mr. Beard was naturally pleased with his success and astral traveled to his fiancée on two other occasions as well. Mr. Beard tried to explain how he was able to leave his body. "Besides exercising my power of volition very strongly, I put forth an effort which I cannot find words to describe. I was conscious of a mysterious influence of some sort permeating my body, and had a distinct impression that I was exercising some force with which I had been hitherto unacquainted, but which I can now at certain times set in motion at will."

Another well-documented case involved Emmanuel Swedenborg (1689–1772). He was attending a party in Goteborg, on July 17, 1759, when a disastrous fire broke out in Stockholm, some 300 miles away. At 6:00 P.M., Swedenborg suddenly went pale and told the other guests about the fire. He restlessly roamed around the house and garden telling the other guests how and where the fire had started, and how it was progressing.

He told them that the home of a friend of his, who he named, had been destroyed and that his own home was in danger. At 8:00 P.M., Swedenborg went outside and exclaimed, "God be praised, the fire is extinguished, the third door from my house!" The next day, Swedenborg was summoned to the Governor's house to repeat his account of the fire. Many people in Goteborg were concerned about the fire because they had friends and relatives living in Stockholm. Several people owned property there as well. It was two days before messengers from Stockholm arrived and were able to confirm every detail of Swedenborg's account. Swedenborg had the ability to astral travel anywhere he wished, and even traveled to the angelic realms. He wrote extensively about his findings there.[12]

In 1918, Ernest Hemingway was a nineteen-year-old soldier serving in Italy. While handing out chocolate to Italian soldiers, he was badly wounded in the legs and had a spontaneous out-of-body experience. "I felt my soul or something coming right out of my body, like you'd pull a silk handkerchief out of a pocket by one corner," he recalled.[13] Hemingway was able to make good use of this experience when he wrote *A Farewell to Arms*. In this book his hero, Frederick Henry, has an out-of-body experience.

One of the most famous astral travelers of all time was Edgar Cayce. He would enter into trance to conduct his medical diagnoses of sick people who may have been thousands of miles away from him. In trance, his vital functions would all slow down until he appeared to be in a near-death coma. Then, what he termed his "finer body" would travel to the subconscious minds of his clients to determine what was wrong with them.

It is interesting to note that Edgar Cayce would not allow anyone to pass anything across his body while he was in the trance state, because they might inadvertently damage or sever the invisible cord that connected his physical body with his finer body.[14] This is the cord that is usually described as the "silver cord."

The ability to astral travel can be extremely useful to you in many ways. You can find out what people really think about you. You can obtain answers to questions that have been puzzling you. You can visit friends and loved ones to see how they are getting on. You can travel the world, and in fact, the entire universe, from the safety of your own home. You can travel backwards and forwards through time. Once you can astral travel whenever you wish, you will never suffer from boredom again.

For many people, the most important aspect of astral travel is that it proves the spirit can survive without the body, which means that death is not the end. The realization of this has enabled thousands of people to eliminate their fear of death. Scientists have demonstrated that, at the moment of death, the body loses between two and two and a half ounces of weight and a mist appears to leave the body in the area of the head. This could well be the astral body and soul of the person beginning their final out-of-body experience.

Almost everyone who has experienced an astral projection, even an involuntary one, has wanted to do it again and again.

Fortunately, it is a skill that anyone can learn. In many ways it is similar to learning to drive a car. Some people take to it naturally and need very few lessons before they are driving safely wherever they wish to go. Other people take longer to learn, but ultimately end up being just as competent as the faster learners. Some people take ages to learn. They might be nervous or timid, or have a poor instructor. However, ultimately, they also learn.

I know from my own experiences with my students that you will be able to astral travel. I was never able to tell by looking at my students which ones would find it easy and which ones difficult, but in time they all learned how to astral travel.

I have included a large number of different methods of leaving the body in this book. This is because I have been unable to find a single method that works for everyone. However, I know that at least one—and in fact probably several—of the methods described here will work for you.

You will find it best to read the entire book before starting on the exercises. Then read the book again more slowly, doing all of the exercises in sequence, even if some of the early ones seem easy. Do not try an experiment in one chapter, then move backwards or forwards through the book and try another. This is particularly the case in Chapter Nine. I have written the book in the order that I know works. It might take a little bit longer to do it this way, but the results will prove extremely worthwhile for you.

Chapter One

Astral Travel Requirements

ASTRAL PROJECTION IS BASED ON THE FACT THAT WE possess two bodies: the physical body that grows, matures, and finally dies, and the astral body, which is a "double" of the physical body. It is this astral body that can, at times, detach itself from the physical body and move away, bearing with it the person's consciousness. In effect, when this occurs, the person is living in the astral body and can look calmly, and in a detached manner, at the physical body he or she has just left.

There are many benefits of being able to astral travel. You will see the world through different eyes. Everything becomes clearer, brighter, and more intense when viewed from the astral body. Most importantly, once you have found that your consciousness can live apart from the physical body, you will realize that your soul can live on, no matter what happens to your physical body. This means that death is not the end, and in fact marks just the start of an even greater adventure.

Most of my students found it relatively easy to learn how to astral travel. However, a number of them experienced difficulties. There was always a reason for this.

Fear was by far the most common cause of failure. We have all experienced fear at times and know how crippling it can be. Many years ago, I was with a group of people who went bungee jumping. We were all keen to do it, and the few who had done it before kept telling us what a wonderful experience it was. However, when we stood on top of the bridge and looked down at the river far below, I am sure all of us felt a little bit scared. Funnily enough, some of the most nervous people volunteered to go first, because they wanted to get it out of the way. I will never forget the feeling in my stomach just before I jumped.

There were twenty of us in the group. Finally, nineteen had jumped. The last person was a man in his early thirties who had been extremely outgoing on the trip to the bridge. I had not noticed when he suddenly became quiet. He allowed himself to have the bungee cord attached and listened intently to what the instructor told him. A few of us yelled out encouragement to him. It looked as if he was going to jump. He swayed slightly and then put out a hand for support. The instructor spoke to him, and again he appeared ready to jump. This time we all remained quiet, though we were all silently willing him to do it. It did not happen. After about five minutes, the bungee cord was untied and he shame-facedly joined us as we went for afternoon tea.

Several people sat with him and told him of their experience, and how they had overcome their fear. He listened and said that he would jump after all. We returned to the bridge with him, but again he could not do it.

Several of my students were like that when it came to astral travel. They wanted to do it, but found that a variety of fears held them back. In my classes I would try to anticipate any potential problems by going through the main fears and answering them.

The most common fear is that the person will not be able to return to the physical body after the astral travel. There has never been a recorded instance of this happening. In fact, the opposite seems to be the case most of the time. Frequently, when you are astral traveling you will suddenly be drawn back into your body, even though you are not ready to return.

Another common fear is that the person will die while astral traveling. While astral traveling we are always connected to the physical body by a long, seemingly elastic cord. If this were cut while you were traveling, you would certainly die, but again, there have been no recorded instances of this happening. The cord is invisible to other people, so it cannot be cut maliciously. Neither can it be cut by rubbing against rough surfaces.

Some people are concerned that their physical body might be taken over by some other entity while they are astral traveling. This is a fine topic for horror movies, but there have been no recorded instances of it ever happening. At the slightest sign of any potential danger to the body, the astral body is instantly returned.

Other people are concerned that their heart might stop or that they could forget to breathe while astral traveling. This does not happen. All the involuntary functions of the body continue normally. It is believed that the body temperature drops very slightly while the person is enjoying an out-of-body-experience, but nothing else changes.

Leaving the physical body and astral traveling is what this book is all about. It is perfectly safe, and there have been no recorded instances of people being unable to return to their physical bodies.

Likewise, if some disaster struck while you were astral traveling, you would instantly return. There is no risk of returning from an astral travel to find that your house burned down while you were out on the astral plane, because, at the first sign of danger, your physical body would force your astral body to return.

I had an experience some years ago in which a car backfired on the street outside while I was astral traveling. The noise was sudden and loud, and I was instantly returned to my physical body. I must confess that I was startled and it took a couple of minutes before I felt comfortable in my physical body. All the same, I was pleased that the return was so rapid, because it proved to me that if anything untoward were likely to happen I would immediately be back and ready to handle the situation.

Some years ago, my wife tried to wake me up on a Saturday morning by shaking me. I did not respond, because I was astral traveling. My wife knew what was happening and went away for a few minutes. When she returned, I awoke easily at the first shake, because by then I was back in my body.

However, if a stranger had walked into our bedroom and shaken me in the same way my wife had, my astral body instantly would have returned to my physical body because of the potential danger. It is interesting that my body can tell the difference between a familiar, non-threatening shake and a potentially dangerous one. This demonstrates that at least part of our consciousness stays behind when we astral travel.

Consequently, your physical body is protected while you are astral traveling. Your superconscious mind goes on the astral travels, but part of it stays behind to protect you.

A final fear is that the person will experience unpleasant things or meet unpleasant entities while astral traveling. This is possible, but if it happens, all the person need do is desire to return to the physical body and he or she will immediately return. Consequently, the astral plane is a great deal safer than the physical one, as we can instantly escape disagreeable situations.

As you can see, all of these common fears are groundless, which means they are exactly the same as most fears that people have. Even though they are groundless, if you suffer from any of them, they will prevent you from astral traveling until you learn to overcome the fear.

Some people find it hard to believe that we can actually be two people inside the same body, and that we have an astral body as well as a physical one. However, we take this fact for granted in much of our conversation. Whenever we refer to "I," we are talking about our spirit or soul that lives within us. When we talk about "me," we are referring to the physical body that is our home during this lifetime. Consequently, we might, for instance, say "I love" or "I feel," and then say "my hand" or "my body."

The *Rig Veda*, the 4,000-year-old holy book of the Hindus, says that we are like a driver in a chariot. The chariot represents "me," the body, while the driver represents the "I," the spirit or universal life-force.

Recognizing that we consist of both the "me" and the "I" can make it easier for some people to successfully astral travel.

In my psychic development classes, many people have told me that they can see the aura of their partners while these people are asleep. Actually, they are not seeing the aura at all, even though it looks as if they are. What they are seeing is the astral double, which moves very slightly out of the body in sleep (Figure 1). In the dream state, the astral body often moves right out of the physical body and floats ten or twelve inches above it.

There are other factors that can prevent you from astral traveling. The first of these is too much food. Eat lightly on the days that you intend to astral travel. When you fill yourself with food your body has to devote all its energies to digesting and processing it. You are more likely to prefer sleep to astral travel.

Almost everyone in the Western world overeats, so you will be doing your body a favor by eating lightly on the days you intend to travel. I am not a vegetarian, but feel

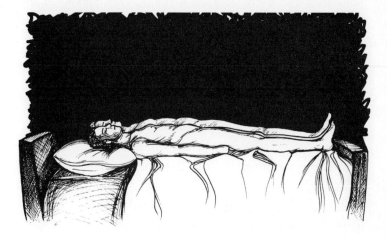

FIGURE 2. *The astral body often floats above*
the physical body in the dream state.

that vegetarians find it easier to astral travel than people
who eat meat. On the days that I want to astral travel, I
either avoid meat or else eat chicken or fish and abstain
from red meats. I also eat as little fatty food as possible.

I find gentle exercise is extremely beneficial as far as
astral travel is concerned. Therefore, I usually go for a
walk before leaving the body. This serves another func-
tion as well. It gets me away from the phone, television,
and other distractions. I can think about the upcoming
astral travel and where I want to go. When I return
home, I am ready to astral project, and also have a pleasant, virtuous feeling from doing something worthwhile
for my physical well-being.

Alcohol and drugs should not be consumed on the
days you intend to astral travel. In fact, both make
astral travel extremely difficult. I know several people

who have astral traveled involuntarily after taking large quantities of marijuana, but found it unpleasant because they had no control over the experience. One kept rocketing into and out of his body continually for three or four hours.

I used to think a glass of wine an hour or two before traveling would be helpful, but I no longer do. You want to be in total control while astral traveling, and even a small amount of alcohol can affect your reactions. The only unpleasant experiences I have ever had in some thirty years of astral traveling occurred after consuming small amounts of alcohol beforehand.

Even cigarettes and coffee can affect your ability to astral travel. Therefore, you should not partake of these for at least three hours before leaving your body.

You should not try to astral travel if you have heart problems or are extremely ill. People often astral travel spontaneously when they are unwell. I am sure you have heard of near-death experiences, in which people feel themselves rushing through a tunnel toward a bright light. These are definitely examples of astral traveling, because these people frequently look back and see their bodies lying in bed or on an operating table.

There is some evidence that extremely ill people can leave their bodies more easily than people who are in perfect health. Sylvan Muldoon, author of three excellent books on astral travel, wrote the first one when he was "so ill that he could not get out of bed, and was never certain but that the next day might prove his last!"[1] However, extremely ill though he was, he still took part in many experiments to verify the facts he included in the book.

Another extraordinary example of the astral traveling abilities of someone who was about to die was related by the German cancer specialist, Dr. Josef Issels, of the Ringberg Clinic in Bavaria. One morning, an elderly woman patient told him that she could leave her body. "I will give you proof," the woman said. "Here and now." There was a brief pause before she spoke again. "Doctor, if you go to Room 12, you will find a woman writing a letter to her husband. She has just completed the first page. I've seen her do it." She then proceeded to describe exactly what she had "seen." Dr. Issels hurried off to Room 12 at the end of the ward and found that the lady had been correct in every detail. When he went back to the woman to question her about her abilities, she was dead.[2]

So far we have discussed the things you should not do. There are also things that you should do before you astral travel.

You must want to astral travel. This desire needs to be strong, as we attract to ourselves what we think about. If you think it would be fun to try astral travel one day, but have no real desire, you are unlikely to succeed.

You also need to maintain a mood of positive expectancy. You need to be relaxed, free of any fears, and looking forward to the experience.

It is hard for many people to relax. If you have difficulty relaxing, you will find it worthwhile to buy a small biofeedback machine. These work on galvanic skin response and are extremely effective in helping people relax. Alternatively, relaxation cassettes are available in many stores. Sitting down quietly, with your eyes closed, listening to the tape, is extremely good for you. The ability to relax completely makes leaving the body that much easier to achieve.

You need to be free of any distractions. Make sure that you will not be disturbed while you are astral traveling. It is a good idea to temporarily disconnect the phone, for instance. You might want to wait until the rest of the family members have gone to bed, so that they will not disturb you.

You need to be reasonably warm, but not hot. The room needs to be at least sixty-eight degrees Fahrenheit (twenty degrees Celsius).

You also need to be free of any constricting clothing. Many people astral travel nude because of this. This does not mean that people can see you naked while you are traveling. If the idea of being seen nude in the astral world concerns you, all you need do is imagine yourself clothed and it will instantly happen.

You need to temporarily forget any worries or problems that are bothering you. I find that the relaxation process does this automatically for me. You might prefer to get rid of them in another way. One lady I know wraps up all her problems and places them in an imaginary refuse bin. On the rare occasions that this does not work, she puts them into a waste disposal unit. One of my students vents his feelings with a vigorous game of squash before astral traveling. It does not matter what you do, just as long as you can place your problems aside until after the astral travel.

You also need to know where you want to go. In the physical world we seldom hop into our cars and simply drive, with no idea of where we are going. We decide that we are going to the mall, or to school, or to a friend's house. Once we have made that decision, it is a simple matter to drive where we want to go.

It is just the same with astral traveling. In fact, it is even easier, because once we are free of the physical body, we simply decide where we want to go and are instantly there. There are no traffic lights, traffic jams, detours, or other delays.

As you can see, the requirements are simple. Most people who astral travel try to lead healthy lives, as they want to be able to astral travel every day. I am sure that you will also choose to do the same, because the benefits and pleasures of astral travel will enhance your life in so many different ways.

Chapter Two

A Few Definitions

OVER THE YEARS I HAVE BEEN ASKED MANY QUESTIONS about astral travel. Most were based on misconceptions and mistaken ideas on what astral travel is. Consequently, before we start astral traveling, it is a good idea to have some idea of what we are doing.

Astral traveling means leaving the physical body behind and moving around in the astral body.

Astral Body

The astral body is a duplicate of the physical body, but is much finer and less dense than the physical body. It is also commonly referred to as the astral or etheric double. Hereward Carrington considered that the astral body was about one-millionth the density of the physical body.[1] He conducted extensive research and concluded that the astral body weighed about one and a half ounces.

When we astral travel, we do so inside our astral bodies. At times we are aware of this. We can see ourselves in our astral body and it feels solid and just like our physical body, except that there are no aches, pains, or diseases. Consequently, astral travel has been a great source of relief and release for people suffering from chronic pain.

Not everyone sees their astral body when out of the body. There also seem to be different ways of seeing ourselves in this state. Some people see themselves as a speck of consciousness racing through space. People who have had near-death experiences frequently astral travel in this form. Many people see themselves astral traveling inside an egg-shaped cocoon.

When you astral travel, your astral body leaves the physical body through the aura in the area between the eyes. This part of the body is known as the *glabella*. The astral body usually returns through the nape of the neck. However, some people find that the astral body simply lifts straight out of the physical body and returns in the same way.

We leave our physical bodies in the astral body when our lives are over. The astral body can sometimes be seen as a small cloud of energy rising from someone just after he or she has ended this incarnation.

The astral body is attached to the physical body by a silver cord.

Silver Cord

The silver cord is a line of light that joins the physical body and the astral body. It usually connects the forehead of the physical body to the navel of the astral body. It is usually whitish to luminous in color, and has been described as a cord, line, chain, strand, string, pipeline, ribbon, connection and magnetic thread. Paul Brunton, in his book *In Search of Secret Egypt*, described it as a "trail of silvery light." Later in the same book he called it "this mysterious physical umbilical cord." Dr. A. S. Wiltse described it as "a small cord like a spider's web."[2] In his book *The Beginnings of Seership*, Vincent Turney also related it to a spider's web when he wrote that it was "very like a spider's cord. It is silver tinged with heliotrope and it extends and contracts as does an elastic cord." Staveley Bulford said that when his astral body was far away from his physical body "the cord looked like a very fine ray of light."[3]

The silver cord is elastic in nature and can be stretched almost indefinitely. Consequently, the farther away the person travels from the physical body, the finer the silver cord becomes. People who have examined the cord closely say that it is made up of a number of strands that are interwoven to create the cord. These individual strands spread out to make a strong attachment at each end.

Some people have described the cord as pulsating with energy and life. Dr. Robert Crookall quoted a young African man who said that every time his cord pulsated it had "a phosphorescent light."[4]

Not everyone reports seeing a silver cord when they astral travel. It is not likely to be noticed unless the person looks back at the physical body he or she has just left. Most people who have seen it turned around to look at their physical body before astral traveling further afield.

The other possibility is that the cord is an impression of a cord linking the two bodies rather than an actual cord. This could explain why some people see it and others don't.

William Gerhardi used the presence of the silver cord to prove to himself that he was astral traveling. "How do I know that I am not dreaming this?" he asked himself. He immediately answered, "Look for the lighted cord behind you!" On another occasion he reported: "I wonder whether I may have died unawares? I…turned round. But the silver cord, faint and thin, was still there."[5]

Many people believe that when the silver cord is severed or broken the person will die. Mr. "G" was present at the death of his wife. He reported that he saw clouds of energy at the instant of death, and that these gradually formed an astral double that hovered horizontally just above her physical body. It was attached by "a cord" that was "suddenly severed."[6] Dr. Burgess, who was also present at the death of Mrs. "G," wrote that Mr. "G" had "not read anything in the occult line" and that in his opinion he could "most positively put aside a temporary acute state of hallucinatory insanity during the time of the vision just recorded."

Dr. R. B. Hout had a similar experience when his aunt died. At first he saw "nothing more than a vague outline of a hazy, fog-like substance." The fog became more dense until he "was astonished to see definite outlines presenting themselves." They formed a human shape that was suspended horizontally a few feet above her physical body. As he watched, he suddenly noticed, intuitively, a silverlike substance that joined the two bodies. "I knew for the first time the meaning of it. This 'silver cord' was the connecting-link between the physical and the spirit bodies, even as the umbilical cord unites the child to its mother." Dr. Hout said, "The cord was round, being perhaps an inch in diameter. The color was a translucent luminous silver radiance. The cord seemed alive with vibrant energy." He could see pulsating light streaming along it. Every pulsation made the astral double stronger and the physical body weaker. As he watched, the various strands of the silver cord snapped until "the last connecting strand of the silver cord snapped and the spirit body was free."[7]

The Astral Plane

The astral plane appears to be a parallel universe to ours. For most people there are no noticeable differences at all. In astral flight they are able to go anywhere they wish and do whatever they want. However, there are some limitations.

For instance, most people are not able to visit a friend and make themselves visible. However, some can. Oliver Fox, author of *Astral Projection*, wrote about the reaction of his girlfriend, Elsie, when he told her about his experiments. She felt that astral traveling was evil and offensive to God. Oliver, a teenager at the time, said that he doubted that she even knew what astral travel was.

"I know more than you think," Elsie replied. "I could go to you tonight if I wanted to."

Oliver laughed and Elsie lost her temper. All the same, that night when he was in bed he "suddenly saw a large egg-shaped cloud of intensely brilliant bluish-white light. In the middle was Elsie, hair loose, and in her nightdress." She stood beside his desk, running her fingers along the top, and gazing at him with sorrowful eyes.

Oliver called her name and she vanished. The next morning Elsie was triumphant because of her success, and gave a detailed and vivid account of Oliver's bedroom. She was correct in every respect except one, Oliver thought. Elsie had felt a projecting ridge on his desk that he was sure was not there. However, when he checked, he found that she was correct. Her fingers had run over the ridge when she stood beside his desk.

This experience encouraged Oliver Fox in his interest in astral travel, and a month or two later he terrified Elsie by astral traveling to her bedroom and standing by her bed. She thought he was there in actuality and was alarmed when she heard her mother coming upstairs to get her out of bed. As the door opened, Oliver disappeared.[8]

Although it is usually not possible to make yourself visible to other people, they are often aware of your presence. Animals, in particular, are very sensitive to astral travelers.

In 1973, research on out-of-body experiences was being done at the Psychical Research Foundation in Durham, North Carolina. Stuart Blue Harary was involved in experiments in projecting himself from one building to another. A kitten with the delightful name of Spirit was in the building he had to project himself to, and it invariably reacted whenever Harary's astral body was present. The kitten was placed on a device that monitored every movement. Spirit was extremely active most of the time, jumping and running around. However, whenever Blue Harary astrally visited the room, the kitten would be quiet and still.[9]

This experiment was taken a stage further in 1978 by Dr. Robert Morris. Four different animals, a gerbil, a hamster, a snake, and a kitten, were placed in cages. Blue Harary, by this time known as Keith Harary, then astral projected to each of the four cages in turn to see what response there would be, if any, from the animals. The gerbil and hamster did not react at all, but the snake became highly agitated. "It started literally to attack," wrote D. Scott Rogo, who was assisting Dr. Morris with the project. "It sort of bit the air viciously for about twenty seconds—twenty seconds which were right in the middle of the time that Keith…claimed to be out of his body and in the cage with the snake."[10] The kitten behaved exactly the same as it had during the earlier experiment. It sat quietly and seemed attentive, but did not make a sound. The experiment was repeated four more times, with the same results.

It can be frustrating to visit a friend while astral traveling and not be able to communicate. However, it is possible to see if everything is going well for the other person. Astral traveling can be a highly effective way of checking on the well-being of friends around the world.

Remote Viewing

This is an area that parapsychologists have been seriously studying for the last twenty-five to thirty years. The term was devised by the research scientists at SRI International (formerly the Stanford Research Institute) in Menlo Park, California, in 1972. In many ways, remote viewing is similar to astral traveling. When you astral travel, you leave the body and travel to anywhere you desire. With remote viewing the person does not leave his or her body. Instead, part of his or her consciousness is sent to a particular place and then reports back on whatever he or she has discovered.

In the early experiments, two people were involved. One, known as the beacon, would randomly choose a target site from a list of sixty choices. He or she would then visit that site and stay there for fifteen minutes. During this time, the person acting as viewer would focus his or her attention on where they thought the beacon might be. The viewer would be directed by an interviewer, who, naturally, also had no idea where the beacon might be.

These experiments were extremely successful. The scientists were amazed to find that people with no previous interest or experience in psychic matters were able to do just as well as people with years of experiments behind them.

Consciousness

In astral traveling and in remote viewing we are moving our consciousness away from our physical bodies and sending it wherever we want it to go. This may sound like a difficult, if not impossible, task. In fact, it is not.

Our awareness is not physical in the first place. We believe that it is contained in our heads, but there is no factual evidence that it is located in our brains. Consequently, when we astral travel we simply move our consciousness into the astral body and go wherever we want to go.

Our consciousness does not have to be in our brains, always assuming that that is where it is. We can place our consciousness anywhere.

You have already astral traveled many times in your dreams. This is called involuntary astral travel, and we will discuss this form of leaving the body in the next chapter, before starting on voluntary astral travel in Chapter Four.

Chapter Three

Involuntary Astral Travel

THROUGHOUT HISTORY THERE HAVE BEEN MANY recorded instances of people who astral traveled involuntarily. Some have traveled in this way for no apparent reason. Mr. P. J. Hitchcock described in the *Psychic Bedside Book* how his son woke up and got out of bed during the night. He walked along a passage and "became aware that something was amiss." When he looked back, he saw what appeared to be a thin cord of light leading from him back into his bedroom. Naturally concerned, he hastily followed the cord back to his bedroom and was amazed to find himself sound asleep in bed. He had no recollection of how he managed to return to his physical body.[1] This is an example of an out-of-body experience during sleep, which occurs to everyone. The unusual aspect of this case is that he woke up while he was astral traveling and became alarmed.

Mrs. Nellie Schlansker of Scotia, New York, had a spontaneous out-of-body experience while wide awake. One day, while sitting with a group of people, she "felt this living part" of her leave her body. She wanted to scream, but couldn't make a sound. Her "other self" stopped about eight feet away and she watched it for some time until it returned to her body.[2]

Fortunately, instances such as these are comparatively rare. Most cases of involuntary astral travel occur when the person is under great emotional stress or is extremely overtired. Some people have reported leaving their bodies involuntarily at the moment of sexual climax, and there are techniques used in the East to make use of the moment of orgasm to trigger a deliberate astral travel.

Most involuntary astral travels occur either in our dreams or in near-death experiences.

Near-Death Experiences

Near-death experiences are the most common examples of involuntary astral travels. Phoebe Payne said that "shock and accident can momentarily drive a person ('double') out of his physical body like an anaesthetic." Carol Zaleski discovered records of near-death experiences in the myths and legends of ancient Greece, Rome, Egypt, and the Near East.[3] A Gallup Poll taken in 1981 showed that some two million American adults had experienced the sensation of being out of their bodies while in a near-death situation.[4]

Approximately nine percent of the people who have a near-death experience involuntarily leave their bodies in this way. This is always experienced immediately after whatever caused them to come close to death occurred. The person is suddenly aware that he or she is floating above or close to the physical body and that his or her consciousness is inside the invisible astral body, rather than inside the physical body.

Most people find it an extremely pleasant, even exhilarating, feeling. They are able to see and hear what is going on in the physical world but at the same time have a sense of the amazing freedom created by being out of the body. In the case of an operation, for instance, the patient is able to float and, without emotion, calmly watch the surgeons working on his or her physical body.

In some cases, people who are out of their bodies have been able to summon help to save themselves. Guiseppe Costa, the Italian engineer, was saved in this way. He had been working hard, studying for his exams, and one night flung himself onto his bed totally exhausted. He had been using a paraffin lamp which he accidentally left on. In his sleep, he knocked over the lamp. Instead of going out, it filled the room with "a black cloud of heavy, acrid gas."

Suddenly, Guiseppe had an out-of-body experience and found himself floating up near the ceiling. Although the room was in total darkness, he was able to see everything surrounded with "phosphorescent outlines." He could even see his body lying on the bed "with the clusters of veins and nerves vibrating like a swarm of luminous living atoms."

He was free and liberated, but at the same time felt enormous anguish as he was not able to open the window because he was separated from his physical body.

He needed help, and immediately thought of his mother who was sleeping in the next room. Instantly, he was in her room. He found that thinking about her caused her to get up and open her window. She then went down the hall, into Guiseppe's room, and groped her way through the smoke until she touched him. Her touch caused Guiseppe's astral body to return and he found himself awake with a parched throat, throbbing temples, and a heart that seemed to be trying to get out of his chest.

This was Guiseppe's first psychic experience, but not his last. Late in life he wrote *Di la della Vita* (*Beyond this Life*), which described his psychic and spiritual development.[5]

A common sensation in near-death experiences is of rushing through a tunnel towards a bright light (Figure 3). Frequently, the person is almost deafened with the noise as he or she races through the tunnel. Usually, the person does not want to return to the physical body after a near-death experience.

A girl I knew in my school days told me of a near-death experience she had after a car accident. She survived the accident but almost died on the operating table as surgeons repaired her damaged body.

"I was swirling through this tunnel," she told me. "I was going really fast—I could feel the speed in my ears. I was heading towards this amazing light. Then I found myself in a beautiful garden, and everything shone with

FIGURE 3. *The sensation of rushing through a tunnel toward a bright light is common in many near-death experiences.*

this incredible light. I noticed that I sort of glowed with it, too. Then some people came towards me, and I knew them all! There was Granny and Uncle Bill. Even Phil, my kid brother, who died when he was eight. They were excited to see me and I was so happy to see them. We were able to speak to each other through our thoughts, and it was fabulous.

"Then the light came. I don't know what it was—God, I guess. It surrounded me and I felt really good, as if this light understood and cared. I saw my whole life flash before me in just a few seconds, and then I was heading back. I thought *I don't want to go back*, but instantly I was back in my body. I tell you that experience changed my life. Everyone says I'm different now and puts it down to the car crash, but that's not it. It's seeing the other side. I'm more caring now."

Her experience is typical of many that I have heard and read about over the years. Although they are relatively common, no one was really aware of them until a young student at the University of Virginia became interested.

Dr. Raymond A. Moody was the first person to bring international attention to the phenomena of near-death experiences. At the age of twenty, his professor told him an interesting story about George Ritchie, a psychiatrist he knew, who died of double pneumonia, but then somehow came back to life. George Ritchie was an army private at the time and was pronounced dead at the army hospital in Abilene, Texas, in 1943. After he had been pronounced dead, and his body covered with a sheet, an alert ward orderly thought he saw Ritchie's hand move. The medical orderly looked at the body a second time and again pronounced him dead. However, after a plea from the orderly he pumped adrenaline into Ritchie's heart. To everyone's amazement, the young private returned to life, and after the war had a distinguished medical career. The part of the story that impressed Dr. Moody most was that George Ritchie reported that while he was clinically dead he had experienced the sensation of passing through a tunnel, and had seen Beings of Light.

Dr. Moody found the story interesting and remembered it when, many years later, a student of his told him an almost identical story about almost dying in a car accident.

Dr. Moody told the stories to his students and they, in turn, shared with him stories of their friends and relatives who had had similar near-death experiences. Many years later, he was able to say: "In any group of thirty (people), I can find someone who has had one or knows someone who has had one."[6]

Dr. Moody carried on with his research and eventually wrote the international bestseller *Life after Life* and other books on the subject.[7]

People were having near-death experiences well before Dr. Moody became interested. One particularly well-known case concerned Dr. A. S. Wiltse of Skiddy, Kansas, who was pronounced dead of typhoid fever in the summer of 1889. Even the local church bells were rung. However, Dr. Wiltse was not dead. A report in the *St. Louis Medical and Surgical Journal* quotes Dr. Wiltse:

"I...discovered that I was still in my body, but the body and I no longer had any interests in common. I looked in astonishment and joy for the first time upon myself...with all the interest of a physician.... I watched the interesting process of separation of soul and body."[8]

In the same article, Dr. Wiltse described his out-of-body experience. He left his body and noticed a man standing by the door of the hospital room. As Dr. Wiltse came closer to the door "his arm passed through mine without apparent resistance.... I looked quickly up at his face to see if he had noticed the contact but he gave no sign, only stood and gazed towards the couch I had just left. I directed my gaze in the direction of his and saw my own dead body.... I was surprised at the paleness of the face.... I know I attempted to gain the attention of the people with the object of comforting them as well as assuring them of their own immortality.... I passed about among them...but found that they gave me no heed. Then the situation struck me as humorous and I laughed outright...how well I feel, I thought. Only a few minutes ago I was horribly sick and distressed. Then came that change called death which I have so much dreaded. This has passed now, and here am I, still a man, alive and thinking, yes thinking as clearly as ever, and how well I feel; I shall never be sick again. I have no more to die."

Almost everyone who has a near-death experience loses any fear of death, because they realize that death is not the end. Another interesting aspect of this experience is that the survivors invariably become more loving and caring.

Carl Jung, the famous psychiatrist, broke his foot in 1944 and then immediately had a heart attack which almost killed him. A nurse told him later that his body had been surrounded by a "bright glow," something she had observed in many people shortly before they died.

Fortunately, Carl Jung did not die. He found himself out in space looking down on the Earth, which was "bathed in a gloriously blue light." He saw the deepness of the seas and the shapes of the different continents. Below his feet was Ceylon (Sri Lanka) and straight ahead was India. He could not see the whole Earth, of course, but "its global shape was plainly distinguishable and its outlines shone with a silvery gleam through that wonderful blue light."

After staring at the Earth for a long while, Jung turned around and saw a huge block of stone, like a meteorite, floating in space. There was an antechamber on this rock, and beside the entrance sat a Hindu in the lotus position. Jung felt great peace, humbleness, and contentment as he stepped onto this huge rock. "I had everything that I was, and that was everything."

Jung was about to pass through into an illuminated room where he felt he would learn the answers to all his questions about the meaning of life when "Dr. H" arrived. This was the doctor who was treating him in the hospital, only now he was "framed by a golden chain or a golden laurel wreath." Dr. H told him that he had no right to leave the Earth yet, and must return. Carl Jung was "profoundly disappointed" and reluctantly returned to the world of the living.[9]

Carl Jung obviously had a near-death experience, but in many ways it was more like an astral travel than the usual "tunnel of light" experience. It shows that near-death experiences can come in a variety of different forms. Carl Jung had a number of other visions before he regained his health. He wrote: "It is impossible to convey the beauty and intensity of emotion during these visions. They were the most tremendous things I have ever experienced . . . . I would never have imagined that any such experience was possible. It was not a product of imagination. The visions and experiences were utterly real; there was nothing subjective about them; they all had a quality of absolute objectivity."[10] This agrees with what most people say about near-death experiences. The entire experience seems to be totally real. There is nothing dream-like about it at all.

Many people have dismissed these near-death experiences as hallucinations. However, the type of experience we have mentioned here is common to people of all countries around the world. Even young children experience them. Dr. Melvin Morse's book, *Closer to the Light*, records his experiences with young children who have experienced leaving their physical bodies when having a near-death experience.

Kim Clark, a nationally known researcher on near-death experiences, was given graphic proof of the reality of these involuntary out-of-body experiences while she was a young psychologist at Harborview Hospital in Seattle.

She was counseling a heart patient by telling her about the different psychological adjustments she would have to make when she left the hospital. But the woman wasn't interested. She wanted to tell Kim that she had left her body and floated above it while doctors frantically tried to restart her heart.

She could see that Kim was skeptical and to prove her case the woman said that there was a shoe on the ledge outside the hospital window. Kim opened the window, but could not see it. The woman kept insisting, so Kim leaned out, but still could not see a shoe.

"It's around the corner," the woman said.

The window was on the fifth floor of the hospital, but Kim bravely crawled around the ledge, and sure enough, there was a shoe, just as the patient had described. It was this incident that started Kim Clark's career in studying near-death experiences.[11]

It was Dr. Melvin Morse who finally demonstrated that near-death experiences occurred only to people who were on the brink of death, and were not the result of sleep deprivation, drugs, or subconscious fears. Dr. Morse and his team of researchers compared the experiences of people who almost died with those of people who were seriously ill, and found that only people who had almost crossed the threshold of death had near-death experiences. Dr. Morse's findings were published in the *American Journal of Diseases of Children* in November 1986.

Dr. Morse also found the area of the brain in which near-death experiences occur, and hypothesized that this location could be the "seat of the soul."

It is interesting to note that very few people who involuntarily leave their bodies during a near-death experience see their astral double. They usually see themselves as a small spark of consciousness. This is still an out-of-body experience. Keith Harary, who was extensively tested by parapsychologists in the 1970s, could astral travel as "an 'apparition,' as a ball or shaft of light, or merely as a point of consciousness dangling in space."[12] These are all different ways in which people can astral travel, and all are equally as valid.

Crisis Visions

There have been many reported cases of people who were visited by an apparition of a friend or loved one at the moment they died. These are obviously instances where the person who died has spontaneously appeared to say goodbye.

I was told a sad example of this by a lady who attended one of my lectures. She had an uncle who lived sixty miles from her home. He was in his eighties, had been widowed for ten years, and lived alone. Frequently, this lady thought she should pay him a visit to see how he was, but she was leading a busy life and never quite got around to it. He was deaf and it was difficult to have a proper conversation with him over the phone.

Finally, she made up her mind that the following day she would bake him a cake and take it over as a surprise. Unfortunately, that morning her son fell off his bicycle and she spent the rest of the day attending to him.

In bed that night, she told her husband that she would visit her uncle on the following weekend. Early the next morning, something woke her up, and she saw a ghost-like apparition of her uncle standing at the foot of the bed. She instantly knew that he had died and she reached over to wake up her husband. By the time he woke, the apparition had gone.

"I'll never forget the sad, lonely expression he had on his face," she told me. When the family went to his home to clean everything up before selling the house, the neighbors all told her how lonely her uncle had been. The neighbors had done what they could to help the old man, but were not aware that he had any surviving family.

"I learned a lot from that," she told me. "Do it now. Not next week, or even tomorrow. If you've made up your mind to do something, do it now."

Edmund Gurney, author of the monumental book *Phantasms of the Living*, said that apparitions could appear from twelve hours before the person died to twelve hours after death. In this book, Gurney described one of the most famous instances of a crisis vision:

Lord Brougham was a leading English statesman. As a child and young adult, he and his best friend G frequently discussed life after death and the immortality of the soul. Finally, they drew up an agreement, written in their blood, which said that whoever died first would appear to the other, and consequently provide proof of life after death.

After college, the young men saw each other infrequently, particularly when G went to India. After a few years, the two men stopped communicating.

In 1799, Lord Brougham was travelling in Sweden with some friends. It was bitterly cold outside and in the evening Lord Brougham enjoyed relaxing in a hot bath at the inn where they were staying. As he was about to get out of the bath, he turned around to look at the chair where he had left his clothes. On the chair, to his amazement, sat his old friend G. "How I got out of the bath I know not," wrote Lord Brougham, "but on recovering my senses I found myself sprawling on the floor. The apparition, or whatever it was, that had taken the likeness of G, had disappeared . . . ." When he returned home to Edinburgh, Lord Brougham learned that G had died on December 19, the day he saw the apparition.[13]

In 1991, Erlendur Haraldson, an Icelandic parapsychologist, published the results of a survey of crisis visions. These visions account for some fourteen percent of all sightings of apparitions. In fact, the figure would be higher if it included apparitions of people who did not die but were involved in some sort of crisis situation. In eighty-five percent of the cases, people seeing the apparition did not realize until later that the person they saw had died. In half of all cases the apparitions were seen within half an hour of the person's death. Finally, it appears that five percent of the population will see a crisis vision at some time during their lives.[14]

In effect, a crisis vision is the deceased person's final astral travel in the astral double of the physical body that he or she lived in during this incarnation.

Sometimes a crisis vision can occur in another form. Perhaps a voice or other sound is heard, or a familiar scent wafts into the recipient's nostrils. Dr. Louisa Rhine conducted a survey of crisis visions and found that by far the greatest number consist of people hearing a familiar voice calling their name.

A tragic example of this was reported in France in 1907. A woman living in Bordeaux was awakened one night by an agonized voice calling out her name three times. She later discovered that her former fiancé, whom she was forbidden to marry, had died during the night and had called out her name from his deathbed.[15]

Dreams

We all astral travel in our dreams, though most people are not aware of it. Dreams of flying are common to people of every culture and time. There is a belief in some primitive cultures that, because the soul wanders during sleep, the body of a sleeping person should never be moved. Another belief is that the astral body hovers over the physical body during sleep, and that we literally fall out of our body as we drift into sleep.

The jerking or sudden sensation of falling that we often experience just before dropping off to sleep occurs when the spirit starts to leave the body but is suddenly jerked back because of unresolved tensions or problems.

Scientists have been studying the relationship between rapid eye movements (REM) and the dream state. In this state, the person's eyes move under the closed lids and brain-wave activity increases. The person also twitches and frequently experiences sexual arousal. Scientists call this the D-state. Scientists have found that when people are awakened in the middle of the D-state, most have very vivid memories of their dreams and can recount them in great detail.

The rest of the time we are asleep is called the A-state. At this time the person lies quietly with few movements, and brain activity decreases, retaining only enough to keep life functions operating. When people are awakened from the A-state, they can recall dreams that seem much like everyday life in the awake state. It has been hypothesized that A-state dreams are actually astral travels.[16] During an average night's sleep, three-quarters of the time is spent in the A-state and one-quarter in the D-state.

When we first go to sleep we pass through what is known as the "hypnogogic stage," which is when the mind and emotions quiet down in preparation for sleep. It is at the end of this stage that the jerking or falling sensation occurs.

Unfortunately, most of the time we do not remember our dreams. We may recall them in a hazy manner when we first wake up, but within an hour or so they are totally lost.

If you want to remember where you astral travel and what you experience in your sleep, you need to prepare for it. In many ways, this is similar to getting ready for an astral travel in the waking state.

First, you have to decide where you want to travel. If you have no destination in mind, you could end up anywhere and possibly have some frightening experiences. Check your destination out in books and magazines if at all possible. Any photographs will help you picture the place in your mind.

Go to bed at your normal time. It is important that you get enough sleep. If you are overtired you will sleep deeply and will have no recall of your dreams. Do not go to bed on a full stomach. This is more likely to produce nightmares than pleasant dreams, and you are again unlikely to remember them.

You are also unlikely to succeed if you are experiencing a large number of worries or are extremely tense or stressed. It is better to wait until your life is running smoothly again before attempting to astral travel. Stress and worry can create involuntary astral travels, but these are generally of short duration and occur while the person is awake.

When you turn out the light, imagine yourself bathed in a white, healing light. Take several deep breaths of this wonderful, pure energy. Allow yourself to relax completely and then visualize the place you intend to visit as you drift off into sleep. By planning what you intend to do in your sleep in this way, your memory of what occurs will improve enormously.

It is a good idea to keep a notebook beside your bed so that you can write down everything you remember as soon as you wake up. I find it helpful to lie quietly for a few minutes, evaluating my dreams before getting up and writing them down. A friend of mine has a small cassette recorder by his bed and recites his dreams onto tape every morning.

A complete progressive relaxation for inducing astral travel in your sleep is included in Chapter Ten.

Many people's first memories of astral traveling occur when they wake up. Oliver Fox, author of *Astral Projection*, experienced his first astral travels as dreams when he was sixteen years old. He found that while dreaming, he could become aware that he was dreaming and then take control over the dream and astral travel wherever he wished. He called this the "Dream of Knowledge," because he had knowledge that he was dreaming.[17] For him, the secret was to keep the critical factor of his mind awake while the rest of his body slept. This may sound like a difficult thing to do, but with perseverance anyone can master it.

Other people who began their astral travels through sleep include Sylvan Muldoon, author of *The Projection of the Astral Body*, and Keith Harary, the psychic who has been tested more than anyone else on his out-of-body experiences.

Some methods of inducing astral projection include almost falling asleep. Robert Monroe writes that when you can reach and "hold the borderland state indefinitely without falling asleep" you are well on the way to leaving the body.[18]

"Lucid dreaming" is the term given to the type of dream that Oliver Fox experienced, in which you are aware that you are dreaming but do not wake up. The most common examples of these are nightmares, but in these instances, the person normally decides to wake up, rather than direct the dream to a different conclusion. Lucid dreaming is something that anyone can learn to do if they are prepared to work at it.

P. D. Ouspensky, the famous Russian mystic, practiced lucid dreaming by deliberately holding on to his conscious awareness until he fell asleep. He found that by doing this, he could maintain consciousness even while asleep, and consequently watch and participate in his dreams.[19]

The easiest way to develop this skill is to concentrate on the dreams you have just before waking in the morning. By then you will have had most of the sleep you need and will probably be half-awake. Remind yourself that dreams are not real, even though they appear to be while you are experiencing them. Then see if you can return to sleep and experience lucid dreaming.

When I do this I find it helpful to imagine that I am flying. I usually fly over cities that I know. For instance, I enjoy flying over London and looking down on famous landmarks that I have visited. However, you could fly anywhere. You may choose to fly over an area that you already know well, or a place that you would like to visit. You may choose an imaginary landscape. It makes no difference. The flying experience will help you drift back to sleep and into a lucid dream.

Dreaming of flying can also help you leave the body and spontaneously astral travel. This was one of Sylvan Muldoon's favorite methods. He believed that whenever you dreamed of flying, you were actually already astral traveling, even though your consciousness was still in your physical body. He found that in this state he could tell himself to wake up out of the body.

Telling yourself that dreams are not real before falling asleep will alert your mind to the numerous incongruities that occur in every dream. When your mind detects one of these during the course of a dream, it can trigger you into a lucid dream that you can then control. You may choose to simply follow the dream to its natural conclusion. You may wish to extend it, or you may decide to change it. Once you are aware that you are dreaming you can do whatever you want with the dream.

Some people create specific triggers to help them turn their dreams into lucid ones. It can be something fairly simple. For example, flying is a common experience in lucid dreams; therefore, you may say to yourself over and over again, "Whenever I find myself flying in my dreams, I will know that I am dreaming." Sexual fantasies are common in our dreams. You can use those experiences in the same way to act as a trigger. Alternatively, you can use a recurring dream as a trigger.

I find that when I go to bed physically exhausted, I am more likely to experience lucid dreams during the night. Emotional problems can also create lucid dreams. At one stage in our lives, when my wife and I were having problems with one of our children, I found that I was having lucid dreams every night. However, I recommend you explore physical exhaustion in preference to emotional exhaustion!

You can also use your lucid dreams to leave the body and astral travel. During a lucid dream, tell yourself to return to the physical body and you will find that you can see yourself asleep under the blankets in your bedroom. From this position, all you need do is tell yourself to leave the body and you will suddenly find yourself floating around the room.

Do not be disappointed if this fails to happen the first time you try it. Keep on trying whenever you have a lucid dream and you will ultimately succeed. A feeling of positive expectancy makes any form of astral travel easier to achieve. Consequently, it is important to keep on trying, confident in the knowledge that ultimately you will succeed.

Dr. Frederick Van Eeden, a Dutch physician and psychologist, was the first person to explore lucid dreams and use them as a springboard to astral travel. He also came up with the term "lucid dreams." He began studying his own dreams in 1896 and began lucid dreaming and astral traveling one year later. He particularly enjoyed flying, visiting and conversing with people who had died, and exploring interesting landscapes. Sometimes he would seem to wake up while astral traveling and could see his astral double standing next to where his wife lay sleeping. He published his discoveries in 1913.[20]

Dreams and out-of-body experiences can also work side by side. In his book *Psychic Empowerment*, Dr. Joe H. Slate tells of a woman who experienced a recurring dream in which her car overturned several times. Eventually, the accident occurred in real life. The woman spontaneously left her body and watched her car overturn several times, exactly as it had done in her dreams. This woman was able to walk away from the accident without injury.[21]

Involuntary astral travels are interesting, but unfortunately we have no control over how and when they occur. In the next chapter we will start learning how to astral travel whenever we wish.

Chapter Four

Getting Started

IT MIGHT SURPRISE YOU TO LEARN THAT YOU HAVE already astral traveled thousands of times in your life. In our dreams we all astral travel. The only problem is that once we are fully awake we usually forget what we have dreamed about.

Many people astral travel in their imagination. I knew a woman who had visited all the famous art galleries in the world in her mind. As she described her experiences in the Louvre, I could hardly keep myself from interrupting her. Even though she denied that she had ever astral traveled, she described the entrance and the various galleries in the Louvre in such detail that I recalled them from my visit there. This lady simply closed her eyes and imagined herself wherever she wanted to be. She never experienced any sensation of leaving her body behind and called what she did "mind traveling."

You have probably done exactly the same when you imagined things in your mind. Mind traveling could explain a number of the common *déjà vu* experiences that people have. This is when you feel that you have been somewhere before, even though that you have not.

I had this sensation at the Temple of Poseidon in Sounion, Greece. I knew what was going to be around every corner, because somehow I had been there before. Originally, I put these feelings down to a partial recall of a past life, but then realized that I had been looking forward to visiting Greece and had astral traveled there several times before making the trip. I had certainly not deliberately chosen to astral travel to the Temple of Poseidon, but may well have visited it in the course of my explorations.

Fortunately, we can test ourselves when we mind travel.

Mind Travel

The basic format of mind travel is very similar to that of astral travel. However, it is much easier to do, which is why we are starting with it.

We start by ensuring that we will not be disturbed for at least an hour. Temporarily disconnect the phone and ensure that the room you will be working in is warm, but not unpleasantly hot. Many people experience losing a couple of degrees of body heat while mind and astral traveling.

Wear loose-fitting, comfortable clothes. Many people prefer to astral travel nude, but this is not necessary with mind travel.

Lie down flat on your back on the floor, or else half-lie on a recliner chair. Lying down on a bed is not a good idea as you are likely to fall asleep. Use a soft pillow if necessary. Cover yourself with a light blanket if you wish. The room should be darkened, but there is no need for it to be pitch black. A table lamp placed a few feet behind you will provide sufficient light.

We now use a progressive relaxation exercise to allow the body to become as physically relaxed as possible. If you already have a progressive relaxation technique, use that. If not, here is one that I find helpful. Originally, I recorded it on tape, but now that I know it by heart, I simply close my eyes and say it to myself. If you record it, bear in mind that a male voice will help you relax more easily if you are female, and a female voice will do the same if you are male. If you do not wish anyone to know what you are doing, it is acceptable to record it in your own voice. Take your time when you record your script and include plenty of pauses between the sentences.

Here is the script:

Take a nice deep breath and close your eyes as you exhale. Allow a wave of relaxation to spread throughout your entire body. Take another deep breath and, as you exhale, allow the pleasant relaxation to spread to every nerve and fiber of your entire body.

It is so pleasant to relax like this, with no cares, no anxieties. Just the pleasant warmth and total relaxation.

As you breathe in again feel the muscles of your feet beginning to relax. Allow the muscles of your toes to relax more and more with every breath you take. Allow that wonderful relax-ation to spread to every part of your feet and up to your ankles, relaxing more than you've ever relaxed before.

Feel that relaxation as it moves up into your calves and into your knees. It's a wonderful feeling. Nothing need disturb or worry you as you go deeper and deeper into this pleasant relaxation.

Allow the relaxation to move into your thighs now. Feel all that tension dissolve and fade away. It's so pleasant, so tranquil, and so, so relaxing.

Double the relaxation in your legs now and then let the relaxation move up into your stomach and into your chest.

Every breath you take makes you feel more and more relaxed, more and more relaxed. It's becoming easier and easier to do with each relaxing breath. Each breath takes you into a deeper and deeper state of total, complete relaxation.

Feel the relaxation move into your shoulders now, and then slowly drift down each arm to the tips of your fingers. Your hands and fingers are so relaxed now, so loose and limp and lazy.

Allow the relaxation to move into your neck. Feel all the tension fade away and enjoy the relaxation moving into every part of your body.

Let the relaxation move into your face. Feel the muscles around your eyes relaxing and then let the relaxation move right up to the top of your head, so that every part of your body is totally, completely, absolutely relaxed.

And in this nice, calm, peaceful state, picture yourself lying on the bank of a stream. You can hear the gurgling of the water as it gently flows past. You can hear the sounds of birds playing up in the trees, and you can feel the gentle touch of a cooling breeze.

In your mind's eye, see yourself get up and walk slowly alongside the stream, watching a leaf gently floating on the water like a little boat as it gets carried away. Soon you can hear the sound of a waterfall, and as you round a bend you see it straight ahead.

Beside it are ten wooden steps leading down to a large, smooth rock below. You place your hand on the handrail and start to go down the steps. A funny thing happens. With each step you take, you double your relaxation, so that by the time you get down to that large, sun-drenched rock you'll be ten times more relaxed than you are now, totally, absolutely relaxed in every part of your mind, body, and spirit.

Ten. Moving down gently, doubling your relaxation.

Nine. Another step, and your relaxation doubles yet again.

Eight. Moving down gently, feeling the gentle spray of the waterfall as you double your relaxation once more.

Seven. Even further now into complete and total relaxation.

Six. Drifting and floating into total relaxation.

Five. Halfway down and feeling as relaxed as a loose, limp rag doll.

Four. Three. Two, and one. Deeper and deeper and deeper into total, complete relaxation.

Feel yourself step onto the nice, warm rock and lie down on its smooth surface. Relaxed. Relaxed. Relaxed and so peaceful. Total, complete, absolute relaxation throughout every part of your body.

Once you have completed the progressive relaxation and are lying, quietly and expectantly, visualize as completely as you can another room in the house you are in.

Picture it as clearly as you can. Do not rush this part of the experiment, because you will be using it to verify your findings later.

Not everyone can see things clearly in their mind. If you find it difficult to picture the room in detail, sense it, even smell it in your mind, if that seems appropriate.

After you have done this, become aware of yourself once more, reclining in a relaxed state. Become aware of your breathing, the temperature of the room, and any sounds that you can hear.

Then tell yourself that you are coming out of this relaxed state, back into the present world, as you count from one to five in your mind. I say this to myself:

> **You are going to return now, back to the present, as you count from one to five. You will feel relaxed, happy, and full of energy, totally restored and invigorated in mind, body, and spirit.**
>
> **One. Feel the energy returning to your body.**
>
> **Two. Feeling wonderful in every possible way.**
>
> **Three. Becoming aware of your surroundings and remembering absolutely everything that happened in the mind projection.**
>
> **Four. Feeling better than you've felt in ages.**
>
> **And five. Eyes opening and feeling wonderful.**

Remain lying quietly for perhaps a minute after opening your eyes. You might feel the need to stretch or relive the pleasant sensations you have experienced.

When you are ready, get up. Take a pen and paper and write down everything you can remember visualizing in the room you visited during the mind projection.

Once you have done that, go through the room and see how accurately you pictured it. You will probably be surprised at the details you recalled. You may find, for instance, that you noticed something out of place in your mind projection and that it is out of place in actuality. This all helps to validate the experience, because otherwise it is hard to determine if you simply recalled the room in your mind, or if your mind actually traveled to the room and surveyed it anew.

Do not do any more experimenting on the day you do this first mind projection. The next time you do it, you can go further afield. You might, for instance, decide to mind project to a friend's house and see what they are doing. Be careful with this. You are doing these experiments to help become a capable astral traveler, not a psychic voyeur. If you find your friend is doing something that you know they would rather you did not know about or witness, withdraw immediately.

Let us suppose that you have a friend called Sonia and you have mind projected to her home. You can clearly see her working in the kitchen. Maybe she is cooking or doing some dishes. Visualize Sonia and the scene as clearly as you can in your mind. Mentally touch her on the shoulder and see if you can attract her attention. It is unlikely that you will be able to do this on the first few attempts, but in time, you will.

When you are ready, return to your own home and count from one to five to return fully to the present.

Call your friend simply to say hello. You may find that Sonia replies that she was just thinking about you. She may even comment that she saw a brief vision of you as she worked in the kitchen.

It does not matter if your friend makes no comments of this sort. Ask her what she is doing and this will confirm what you saw.

Do not worry if your mind picture was completely wrong. You may have visualized her in the kitchen, when she was actually asleep in bed or out with friends. It takes time to get good at these things. Simply try again on another occasion.

After you have successfully done this several times, use mind travel to locate a friend who is not at home. When you open your eyes afterward, take note of the time and then check your findings with your friend.

You may have to be careful what you tell your friend. A friend of mine got very upset when I tracked her down in this way, because she thought that I was spying on her. If your friend is not receptive to mind and astral travel, it might be better to say, "I phoned you this afternoon, but you were out," and see what your friend says. If he or she replies that they were visiting the place you mentally saw them in, you will know that you were successful. Even if they say they were somewhere else, you may still have succeeded, because they may have visited a number of places on their outing.

Now it is time to take this exercise still further. Make arrangements to visit a place that you have not been to before. This might consist of visiting a different town, or the home of a new acquaintance, or perhaps even an office where you will be going for a job interview.

After completing the progressive relaxation part of the exercise, visualize yourself visiting this new place. See it as clearly as you can, and see yourself doing all the things you will be doing when you visit. Naturally, you will be able to see how successful you were when you make your visit. You will probably be pleasantly surprised at how accurate your visualization was.

Not long ago, I was the guest speaker at a service club. Just for fun I did this visualization exercise a couple of nights before attending the meeting. I was surprised to discover that this club met in what appeared to be a church hall. When I went there to speak I found that this was the case. My visualization was almost completely perfect. However, what I thought was a room divider on one side of the room actually turned out to be a large number of stacked chairs.

You will find that often you will be partially successful. You may correctly determine the shape of the room and the type of furnishings, but perhaps have the desk in a different location. The color of the carpet may be wrong, even though everything else is correct.

It used to concern me that I couldn't visualize the location perfectly every time, but there is no point in worrying about it. We all see the world from our own particular perspective, and continue to do this even when we are using visualization techniques. I am sure you have experienced the sensation of revisiting a place and discovering something that you had not noticed before. As we do not always see everything perfectly when we visit a place physically, we certainly cannot expect to do so when we mind travel there.

Mind travel provides excellent practice in the necessary techniques to achieve astral travel. You need to be able to relax, concentrate, visualize, and remain mentally alert. As you can see, mind travel utilizes all of these.

Some of my students were so happy with their skill at mind traveling that they did not continue on to full astral traveling. Mind traveling can be extremely useful, but most of the time I prefer to astral travel. We will start our preparations for astral travel in the next chapter.

Chapter Five

The Astral World

WHEN YOU ARE OUT OF THE PHYSICAL BODY, YOU ARE free to go anywhere and do almost anything you wish. You can explore places you would never get to in normal life. Have you always wanted to go to Outer Mongolia? All you need do is ask to go there once you are out of the body and you will instantly find yourself there.

You are not restricted to the Earth, either. You can explore Mars, Venus, and anywhere else you desire to go. Naturally, you will want to start slowly by investigating places near home, but there are no outer limits to how far you can go.

You can also travel through time, backward and forward. Have you always wondered what life must have been like in the time of Henry VIII? Go back there and find out for yourself! Do you want to see what life will be like 100 years from now? Go forward through time and experience it for yourself. Cornelius Agrippa, in Book Three of his *Three Books of Occult Philosophy*, reported that a philosopher named Atheus was able to astral travel into the future and return "more learned."[1]

You will remember that I said you can do almost anything. However, you are traveling in the astral world, so you are not experiencing the physical world but the astral replication of it. Consequently, there are limits, both natural and self-imposed. Scientific tests have demonstrated that people can astral travel to different places and read and remember a message to bring back as evidence. Consequently, it would appear that there is nothing to stop you from astral traveling to a locked room and reading the questions—and answers—for a test you have to take tomorrow. In practice, it is not that easy. It is possible to read a sheet of paper while astral traveling, but it is not possible to open a book or turn over pages. If the test paper is inside a drawer, you will not be able to read more than the first page.

In his book *Astral Projection*, Oliver Fox described how he astral traveled in his sleep to see an exam paper the night before the test. He was able to recall two questions that were in the paper. One was a question that was likely to be included anyway, but the other was a question that had not been asked on this particular exam for many years. He explained that he was unable to recall more than two questions as he found that "the print seems clear enough until one tries to read it; then the letters become blurred, or run together, or fade away, or change to others."[2] Oliver Fox did not attempt to repeat this experiment, because it made him him feel uneasy.

There are also self-imposed limits brought about by your own personal standards and ethics. At times, in your astral travels, you will encounter situations that other people would prefer you did not see or know about. You must use your own standards of behavior to decide what you do when this happens. Do you hang around and watch, or do you quietly move away?

I have found that people who astral travel for voyeuristic or selfish reasons invariably suffer as a result. There are a lot of different entities in the astral world and low-grade entities seem to attach themselves to people who astral travel for the wrong reasons.

This brings us to another important requirement for astral travel. You must have a reason for astral traveling. Yes, it is fine to occasionally go off on a trip and flit around the astral plane, but most of the time you should have a specific purpose in mind.

This purpose goes a long way to explain the involuntary cases of astral travel, in which people suddenly find themselves out of their bodies. This can be a terrifying experience for people who have no previous knowledge or experience of the subject. If these people have a definite need or desire to go somewhere or to do something, they can spontaneously astral travel in their sleep, as we all do. The problems arise if they wake up in the course of traveling.

Consequently, if your need to astral travel is extremely strong, you will find it much easier to leave your body than will someone else who is merely curious.

A cousin of mine was concerned about her daughter, who was living thousands of miles away in Turkey. Her daughter was a wonderful letter-writer and every week my cousin received a long, newsy letter. One week no letter arrived. My cousin put this down to the vagaries of the postal system, but she became concerned when another week went by without a letter. She phoned her daughter, but the person who answered the phone could speak no English. Becoming more concerned as each day passed, my cousin found it hard to sleep. Finally, almost four weeks after receiving a letter from her daughter, she managed to drift off into a restless sleep.

In her sleep, she astral traveled to her daughter and found her and her partner enjoying a vacation in the mountains. My cousin returned to her body and went into a sound sleep that lasted twelve hours. Shortly after she woke, her daughter phoned her to see if everything was all right.

"Mike and I were trekking across country and I suddenly saw you," she said. "As soon as we got to a place where there was a phone I called, but there was no answer. Is everything okay?"

My cousin originally thought that she had dreamed about her daughter, but when she learned that she had correctly seen the cross-country trek in the mountains, and that her daughter had seen a vision of her, she realized that she must have astral traveled. In this case the need was so strong that my cousin astral traveled to her daughter to find out for herself if everything was all right. After she had reassured herself that her daughter was fine, she had fallen into such a deep sleep that her daughter's earlier phone call had failed to wake her.

A day or two later a letter arrived from her daughter, saying that she was going on vacation and that she might not hear from her for a week or two. Unfortunately, this letter had been posted from a post box they had passed on their way to the mountains, and it had taken much longer to arrive than usual.

It is wonderful to be able to keep an eye on loved ones in this way. Some thirty years ago, I was sharing a house with several other people in London. One of them always said, "Good night, Dad" out loud before going to bed, because his father astral traveled every night to check on his children, who were scattered around the globe. My friend could always tell when his father was present in the room.

Sometimes people become visible while astral traveling. I am not sure if my friend in London ever saw his father, even though he knew when he was present, but my cousin was certainly very visible to her daughter, even in the mountains of Turkey.

It is possible that a number of ghost sightings that have been reported are actually glimpses of people who are astral traveling.

Bilocation

There are many recorded instances of *bilocation*, which is the word used to describe a situation where one person is seen in two places at the same time. Bilocation could well be a result of people seeing a person's astral double as well as his or her physical body. One well-documented example occurred on September 21, 1744. On September 17, Alphonse de Liguori, a well-known, prominent Naples businessman, was languishing in prison in Arezzo. He stopped eating and lay quietly in his cell for five days. When he got up on the fifth day he told his jailers that on the previous day he had been to the death-bed of Pope Clement XIV. His presence at the bedside was confirmed, proving that he had actually been in two places at the same time, even though the two towns were four days' traveling distance from each other.[3]

One of the strangest instances of bilocation involved William MacDonald who, on July 8, 1896, was appearing in court charged with attempting to burglarize a house on Second Avenue in New York City. Several people had seen him "bumping around" in a room and attempting to leave with valuable items. When the witnesses tried to seize him, he managed to escape, but all of them had had a good opportunity to see him and were easily able to identify him again.

At his trial, Professor Wein stood up as a witness for the defense and said that at the time of the attempted burglary, William MacDonald was on the stage of a vaudeville house more than five miles away from the scene of the crime, and several hundred people had seen him there! William MacDonald had been an audience volunteer at a hypnotism show that Professor Wein had presented that night. Professor Wein explained to the court that the "physical Mr. MacDonald" never left the stage, but that it "may have been a non-physical image of Mr. MacDonald that the residents of the house on Second Avenue saw."

Despite intense cross-examination by the prosecuting attorney, the jury found William MacDonald not guilty.[4]

An equally strange occurrence concerned Mademoiselle Emilie Sagée in Livonia during the 1840s. Despite being an excellent teacher with impressive qualifications, she was dismissed from at least nineteen schools. This was because her double upset her students by constantly appearing to them. Usually, the double imitated Mlle. Sagée's movements and stayed close beside her. However, it was also capable of moving around by itself. One day, the double would stay close to the blackboard, the next it might sit quietly in a corner. Sometimes it wandered through the school grounds on its own. As the double became clearer and more visible, poor Mlle Sagée became more rigid in manner and feeble in health.[5]

There are many instances of bilocation recorded by the Catholic church. One of the most famous instances concerned St. Anthony of Padua, who was preaching at a church in Limoges in 1226. He suddenly remembered that he was supposed to be conducting a service at a monastery at the other end of town. He pulled his hood over his head and knelt down for several minutes while his congregation waited. At this exact moment, at the other end of town, the monks saw St. Anthony come out of his stall in the chapel and give a reading before abruptly disappearing.[6]

The ability of some people to see others who are astral traveling is a good reason not to use this skill to eavesdrop on others, as you have no way of knowing if they can see you or not, unless they react.

The "Wilmot case," originally recorded in the *Proceedings of the Society for Psychical Research*, shows that someone who is astral traveling can sometimes be seen by someone else who is in no way connected with the traveler.

In October 1863, Mr. Wilmot was returning home to Bridgeport, Connecticut from a business trip to Liverpool. On October 3 a severe storm began that lasted for nine days. On the evening of the eighth day, Mr. Wilmot was asleep in his stateroom in the City of Limerick and dreamed that his wife came to the door of his cabin, dressed in a nightgown. At the door she noticed that another man was sharing the stateroom. She hesitated for a moment before coming over to Mr. Wilmot. She caressed and kissed him and then quietly left.

When Mr. Wilmot awoke he found Richard Tait, his fellow passenger, staring at him.

"You're a pretty fellow," Richard said. "You're a pretty fellow to have a lady come and visit you in this way."

Mr. Wilmot demanded an explanation, and discovered that the man had seen everything that he remembered from his dream. Richard had been startled when a woman wearing a nightgown appeared at the stateroom door. He assumed that it must be Eliza, Wilmot's sister, who was also on board the ship, and that she had come to her brother's stateroom because of some emergency. However, as she entered the cabin he could see that she was a woman he had never seen before. The woman hesitated when she saw Richard looking at her, but seemed to choose to ignore his presence. She walked over to Wilmot and began kissing him. In 1863 this behavior was preposterous and brazen. Richard gazed in amazement at this strange woman who seemed heedless of her reputation.

Richard Tait was not satisfied with Wilmot's unbelievable explanation. He sought out Eliza Wilmot the next morning to see if she had visited her brother during the night. Eliza was shocked at what she considered his improper suggestion. Richard apologized and confessed to being "a very puzzled man."

When the ship reached Bridgeport, Mrs. Wilmot asked her husband, "Did you receive a visit from me a week ago Tuesday?"

On the night that the storm began to abate, Mrs. Wilmot lay in bed, worried about her husband because there had been a lot of talk about shipwrecks. About four in the morning, she decided to visit her husband. She astral traveled across the stormy sea and onto the ship.

"Tell me," she asked her husband. "Do they ever have staterooms like the one I saw, where the upper berth extends further back than the under one? There was a man in the upper berth who looked straight at me, and for a moment I was afraid to go in, but soon I went up to the side of your berth, bent over you, kissed you, pressed you in my arms, and then I went away."

Mrs. Wilmot's description of the stateroom was perfect, because it was at the stern of the ship and the berths were not on top of each other.[7]

Doppelgangers

A *doppelganger* is a human double, and is closely related to bilocation and astral travel. *Doppelganger* is a German word, but seems to be far better known than the English word *autoscopy*, which also means "human double."

It can be a highly disturbing experience to unexpectedly come face to face with your astral double. Guy de
Maupassant told a friend how annoying it was to always
find his double sitting in his armchair whenever he
returned home.

Dr. Edward Podolsky wrote an article about doppel-
gangers in the April 1966 issue of *Fate* magazine, and
included accounts of a number of recorded instances.
For example, Mr. Samuel V of Kansas City, Missouri,
was gardening one Saturday afternoon, and every movement he made for more than two hours was duplicated
exactly by his double.

Mrs. Jeanie P found her double beside her one
evening when she was applying make-up. Her double
was doing the same. Mrs. P was curious and reached out
to touch her double, and at the same time the double
reached out and touched her.[8]

One explanation of doppelgangers is that they are
simply a projection of past memories. However, there
have also been a number of recorded instances where
the person saw themselves in the future.

The most famous instance of this concerned the great
German writer Johann Wolfgang von Goethe. He had
been visiting his friend Frederika in Strassburg. As he
rode away he passed a double of himself, wearing
clothes of light gray with gold lace that Goethe had not
seen before. However, eight years later, when again visiting his friend, Goethe suddenly realized that this time
he was wearing the same clothes he had seen his double
wearing years earlier.

There has been very little research into doppel-gangers. James Hewat McKenzie (1870–1929), founder of the British College of Psychic Science, had what must have been an amusing experience in hindsight when he attempted an experiment. McKenzie had strong views on most subjects and spoke his mind freely. He felt that alcohol and other drugs had a deleterious effect on the etheric body as well as the physical body. Although he was strongly opposed to the demon drink, he tested his theory on one occasion by deliberately getting drunk. He then went out into the street for a walk. He glanced across the road and saw himself walking on the opposite sidewalk. Thinking that he must have spontaneously left his body, he crossed the road to return to his body, and carried on walking. When he looked back at the other side again he found that he was still walking along the street on the other sidewalk as well. He panicked because, in his drunken state, he did not know which was his physical body and which was the astral.[9]

There is one major difference between an out-of-body experience and a doppelganger. The double that the person sees does not contain his or her conscious-ness. The person is always aware that it is a double he or she is observing, and that the real person contains the conscious awareness. In an out-of-body experience, the consciousness is in the astral body, not the physical body that is left behind.

Teleportation

Teleportation is the sudden transportation of a person or object from one place to another. There are many accounts of teleportation in the myths and legends of many cultures, and there are also a number of reported instances that have been verified and confirmed genuine at the time.

Probably the most astounding instance occurred in October 1593, when a strangely dressed soldier suddenly appeared among the sentries guarding the Plaza Mayor in front of the palace in Mexico City. The soldier was wearing what appeared to be a guard's costume, but it in no way resembled what the other guards were wearing. The man was dazed and stared around him with disbelieving eyes.

He told the soldiers: "My name is Gil Perez. I was ordered this morning to guard the doors of the Governor's Palace in Manila. I know very well that this is not the Governor's Palace and this is certainly not Manila. Why or how that may be, I know not. But here I am, and this is a palace of some kind, so I am doing my duty as nearly as possible."

Perez could not believe that he was in Mexico City, thousands of miles away from home. The religious authorities quickly imprisoned him as an agent of the devil, but no amount of questioning could make him change his story.

Fortunately for him, a galleon arrived from the Philippines two months later. A government official on board recognized Perez and testified that he had seen the palace guard in Manila just before he set sail for Mexico. The Holy Office believed him and declared that Perez was an innocent victim of the devil, and allowed him to return to the Philippines.[10]

There is no explanation for events such as this. It appears that Perez must have involuntarily left his body, astral traveled, and then somehow turned his astral body into a physical body some thousands of miles away from home.

You now have all the background information that you need to successfully astral travel. In the next chapter we will make our first visit to the astral plane.

Chapter Six

Your First Astral Travel

YOU ARE NOW READY TO EMBARK ON YOUR FIRST astral travel. It is an experience that you will never forget and will want to recapture time and time again.

Just a few things are out of your control. Do not attempt to astral travel in intensely humid conditions or when an electrical storm is in progress. Some people say that you can astral travel safely in stormy conditions if you immerse your right hand in a bowl of water for several minutes beforehand. I would rather not take the risk, and would delay any astral travels until the storm passes.

As with mind travel, choose a time when you will not be disturbed or interrupted. I prefer to wait until the rest of the family has gone to bed. At that time of night the phone is unlikely to ring, and I can spend as much time as I wish in the astral world, unless I am suddenly pulled back into my physical body. Yram, author of *Practical Astral Projection*, used to wake up early in the morning to astral travel. It makes no difference what time of day or night you choose, just as long as you know you will not be disturbed.

Make sure that you have eaten lightly during the previous twenty-four hours. Vegetables and fruits are the best foods to eat on the days you astral travel. If you must eat meat, eat as little of it as possible. Avoid high protein and fatty foods.

Sylvan Muldoon, author of *The Projection of the Astral Body*, recommends deprivation. He feels that you are more likely to leave the body if you are feeling hungry or thirsty. I found the opposite to be the case. When I tried to follow his suggestion I was so preoccupied with my feelings of thirst that I could not leave the body. I eat lightly, but am not starving or thirsty.

I think a willingness to let go of mundane, earthly matters is a much better way of achieving success than deprivation. Most people in the Western world find it extremely hard to let go. We sit down to relax and then start thinking about all the things we should be doing. We think about household chores, conversations we've had, accounts we need to pay, and so on. All of these things need to be put aside before we can successfully leave our bodies.

Many people astral travel from their beds. This is logical, because almost all of the involuntary astral travel we do while we are asleep is done from our beds.

However, for the first few times you astral travel it is better to do it from a comfortable, recliner-type chair or a long couch. The reason for this is that we associate "bed" with "sleep," and it is a shame to fall asleep while relaxing before starting an astral travel. I prefer a recliner chair to a couch, because I find it easier to leave the body from a relaxed sitting position than I do when lying down completely.

Before you start, place pen and paper nearby, so that you can record your impressions as soon as you return. Sometimes you will find your astral trips so exciting, intense, and thrilling that there is no way in the world that you could ever forget them. However, the opposite can also occur, and the memory can fade rapidly, just like a dream. Yram recorded an occasion when he had every detail of his trip clearly in his mind, but all memory of it vanished just as soon as he put pen to paper.[1]

You may wish to perform a small ritual to protect your physical body while you are away. I have never experienced a situation where I needed this protection, but it is an additional safeguard that provides security and may be useful someday. This ritual is known as "psychic protection."

There are many ways to protect yourself. Salt and water are especially useful. Salt is a crystal that represents the element earth. Water represents the psychic world. Consequently, a bath in water that has a small amount of salt dissolved in it can provide excellent protection. Normally, of course, we have a bath to clean ourselves. If we are having a bath as a ritual of protection, we need to remain aware the whole time we are bathing that this is the purpose of it. When you get out of the bath, dry yourself with a rough towel and either astral travel nude or wearing fresh, loose clothing.

You can also use the water and salt in different ways. You might want to place a teaspoon of salt in each of the four major directions around the area you are going to travel from. You can then sprinkle water in a large circle to provide a ring of protection. A friend of mine dissolves salt in water and sprinkles that in a circle using a squeeze bottle, which eliminates the need for salt in the four directions.

An acquaintance of mine lights four white candles, which are placed in the four major directions, and uses these for protection. A woman who attended some of my psychic classes makes the sign of the cross in each direction and says a short prayer when she lies down.

A method that I find very useful is to imagine myself surrounded by a pure white light. I visualize this light as not only surrounding me, but actually permeating every cell of my body as well. Part of this light of protection goes with me on my astral travels, while the rest stays with my physical body.

Most of the time, protection is not necessary, but it is a useful safeguard and you should perform some sort of rite of protection if you feel any uneasiness at all about leaving your physical body behind.

The room needs to be comfortably warm, at least sixty-eight degrees Fahrenheit (twenty degrees Centigrade). You should wear light, non-restrictive clothing. You may wish to travel nude, and this is fine, too. Cover yourself with a light rug or blanket.

Keep your arms and legs uncrossed. The reason for this is that when we cross our arms and legs we are subconsciously protecting ourselves and holding back. We want to do the opposite to successfully leave the physical body, so it is important to keep your limbs uncrossed.

Tell yourself that, after the progressive relaxation, you are going to leave the physical body and astral travel. Repeat this thought over and over like a mantra for a couple of minutes. This helps impress it in your inner mind.

You will need a purpose for the trip. This is easy the first time. Your purpose is simply to leave your physical body and to float a maximum of a few yards from it. It is important not to leave the room on your first trip.

Go through the progressive relaxation exercise that you use for mind travel. When you are totally relaxed, become aware of your breathing. You should be taking quiet, deep, slow breaths.

Become aware of your physical body lying down wherever it is. Become aware of the room and any outside sounds. Become aware of your consciousness. Your conscious mind should be relaxed and at ease, though a sense of anticipation is bound to be present as well.

Think of the purpose of this astral travel and how important it is for you to do it. Gently will yourself to leave your physical body. This is not easy. Your mind needs to be relaxed, but it also needs to be exerting your will to leave the physical body behind. Tell yourself that you are doing this experiment to improve your life and to enhance your potential. It is important for you to leave the body.

Direct your attention to your forehead and allow your conscious mind to move out of the body at this point. You will probably experience a sense of sinking or floating as this happens. You may feel yourself vibrating or shaking all over. You may experience a tickling sensation on your face, as if someone is brushing a fine feather over it. Try to simply go with the flow when any of these things happen, and allow yourself to slip out of the physical body.

You may find that this occurs smoothly and easily the very first time you try it. On the other hand, it may take several attempts before you discover that you have left the physical body. The biggest problem is that most people panic as soon as they feel the sinking or floating sensation, and this immediately brings them back, fully alert, into their body.

I am sure that you have experienced a sensation of falling, just before you pass into sleep. This is a common occurrence, but it creates a feeling of panic and we instinctively jerk our way out of it. Many people do exactly the same with the sinking feeling. When you start to feel that you are sinking through the surface of whatever you are lying on, regard it as a positive sign. Enjoy the sinking feeling, rather than fighting against it. In fact, if you can intensify the feeling in some way, it will make your first astral travel so much easier to achieve. I realize that this is easier said than done.

I learned to water ski the same summer that I first astral traveled. I found that I could get up on the skis, but then instinctively pulled on the rope, which made me fall over. As soon as I learned not to pull on the rope, but to simply let the rope pull me, I was able to water ski.

It is just the same with leaving the body. Simply allow it to happen. The very slightest bit of resistance on your part will bring you straight back into your body.

Once you have astral traveled once, this will cease to be a problem, as the experience will be so exciting and exhilarating for you that you will immediately want to do it again. As with most things, the first time is the hardest.

I find it helpful to tell people to make their minds as still as possible, to simply concentrate on their breathing and to will themselves to leave the body.

Some people find that they can achieve this in a matter of seconds. For other people it might take several minutes. It makes no difference how long it takes. Naturally, it is wonderful if you manage to leave the body on your very first attempt, but it does not matter in the long term if it takes you six months. When you first learned to drive a car, you probably went through a stage during which you felt it was going to be impossible to ever learn to drive. Then, probably quite suddenly, you made a major breakthrough, and now you can drive easily anywhere you wish, without even thinking about the process. Astral travel is much the same. It is a process that needs to be mastered, and the length of time this mastery takes varies from person to person.

If you fail to leave the body on the first occasion, set aside some time on the next day to go through the procedure again. Make it part of your routine and do it every day, until—suddenly, when you least expect it— you will have left your body.

Let's assume that you have successfully left your body and you are now floating above your physical body. Look down at your body and see how tranquil and peaceful it looks. Mentally wish yourself to travel to a certain corner of the room. Before you can properly formulate the thought you will be there.

Feel the walls and see how solid or soft they appear. This will depend on how solid an astral double you have created. Do not worry about this now. Simply experiment. Use one hand to feel different parts of your body. In your astral state they will seem quite firm.

Try visiting each corner of the room in turn and note how you can travel from one corner to another instantaneously just by thinking about it.

Finally, visualize yourself returning to your physical body, and again, instantly, you will be there. Sometimes this return is smooth and gentle, but at other times it can seem rough and violent. I would compare it to the feeling you have of reaching the ground after a parachute jump. Even with a smooth landing, there is a definite jarring sensation.

You should not experience this with your first astral travel, because you have stayed within the room. Generally speaking, the further away from your body you are, the greater the jarring effect of the return. I have never experienced anything nearly as severe as what happened to Sylvan Muldoon when he was twelve years old and returned from his first astral travel. He experienced a penetrating pain as if his body had been split open from head to foot.

Whenever possible, I avoid a painful return by willing myself back to the room where my body is, and then telling myself to return to the body. However, this is not always possible, and frequently you will find yourself back in the body long before you intended to return.

Once you have returned to the body, lie as quietly as possible for a minute or two. This is particularly important if your return was harsh.

Become aware of your surroundings and what you have achieved. Count from one to five, open your eyes, and stretch.

As soon as you get up, take pen and paper and jot down your thoughts and feelings about this first astral travel. This may not seem important at the time, but if you do it religiously, you will find that you gradually build up an extremely valuable record that will become more and more useful to you as time goes by. For instance, you may discover a common theme or thread running through your accounts. When you recognize this, you can deliberately explore the subject further in your later astral travels.

Once you have successfully astral traveled, you will want to repeat the experience as quickly as possible. You may feel resentful that you stayed inside the room, rather than going on to explore the great big world beyond. You will feel excited that you have achieved it and want to know if you can do it again.

Wait twenty-four hours before doing it again. Astral travel uses up psychic energy, and a break of twenty-four hours gives your system time to build itself up again. Once you become used to astral traveling, you will be able to leave your body several times a day, one trip virtually right after the other. For the first few times, though, allow sufficient time for your body to restore itself before traveling again.

The other advantage of this is that it gives you plenty of time to think about what you have achieved. You will probably want to tell everyone about it. Be careful about doing this. Some of your friends will be happy for you, but others won't. Some people will think that you are simply fantasizing. Others may feel that you should be locked up! Your immediate family may become worried that at some stage you'll be trapped on the astral plane and won't be able to return. No matter what you say to them, these fears will remain.

I know a lady who is terrified that she will wake up to find her husband dead, only to find, after he is buried, that he was simply astral traveling and now has no body to return to. This is quite impossible, but is a fear that some people have.[2]

You may be fortunate and have a few like-minded people with whom you can discuss your astral travels. If so, talk freely with them about it, but keep as quiet as possible about your experiences with people who are less open-minded.

Later on, when you have more experience, you will be able to talk about it more openly, and even demonstrate your abilities. At this stage, though, cherish what you have achieved but be careful with whom you discuss it.

Chapter Seven

Advanced Astral Travel

We will assume that it is now at least twenty-four hours since your first out-of-body experience. You are probably still feeling excited about what you achieved and can hardly wait to do it again.

Think carefully about what you want to achieve on your astral travel this time. Certainly, you will want to explore further than your room. Maybe you would like to set up a simple test for yourself. A good one is to ask someone to write a few numbers on a piece of paper which is placed somewhere in their room. During your astral travel you would visit their room and read the numbers. This is a test that scientists used extensively during the 1970s with such super-psychics as Keith Harary and Ingo Swann to prove the validity of astral travel.

Dr. Charles Tart, a California parapsychologist, recorded a series of tests he conducted with a young woman in which she was asked to astral travel and read a series of numbers written on a card and placed on top of a cupboard, well above normal eye level. The woman slept in the laboratory for the four nights during which the tests took place. She did not astral travel on the first night. She succeeded in leaving her body on the second night but was not able to get high enough to see the card. She astral traveled again on the third night but went out of the laboratory and did not try to read the card. Finally, on the last night, she read the number and was able to give the scientists the correct number: "25132."[1] The odds of her choosing this number by chance are just one in one hundred thousand.

In 1973, Ingo Swann was carefully tested at the laboratories of the American Society for Psychical Research in New York. Dr. Karlis Osis conducted much valuable research into the out-of-body-experience here. In one test, Ingo Swann was asked to draw a sketch of the contents of a cardboard box that was suspended from the ceiling of the laboratory some ten feet above the floor. The box contained a red, heart-shaped piece of paper glued to a white backing, and a black, leather-sheathed letter opener.

Ingo Swann sat in a chair and concentrated on leaving his body. His every move was observed and evaluated by scientists and recorded by a television camera. After several minutes with his eyes closed, Ingo Swann returned to his body and drew an "asymmetrical elliptical figure" and a shape that resembled the letter opener. He also correctly labeled the elliptical figure as "red" and the letter opener as "black."

This was just one of a series of tests that Ingo Swann undertook. In one of the tests Ingo Swann was successful eight times in a row. The odds against this occurring by chance are one in forty thousand![2]

Ensure that the conditions are as similar to your first trip as possible. Take your time doing the progressive relaxation. I know from my own experience that when you are in too much of a hurry to escape from your physical body, you fail to relax sufficiently and consequently may not be able to astral travel.

Take your time in relaxing. There is no need to hurry. The quieter and more relaxed you are, the easier it is to leave the body.

Usually, it is much easier to leave the body the second time. By this time the fear of the unknown that we all experience is completely gone, and will have been replaced with a sense of anticipation.

When you complete the progressive relaxation, imagine yourself sinking into a state of nothingness, and suddenly you will find yourself outside your body, probably floating a foot or so above your physical body. Visualize yourself standing up and you will instantly move from a horizontal to a vertical position.

Again visualize yourself in a corner of the room, and instantly you will be there. Take time to have a good look at your astral body. Visualize yourself in a variety of different clothes and notice that the moment you think of them, you are wearing them.

FIGURE 4. *Visualize your astral body in a standing position.*

This time you may notice a thin, silver cord connecting the astral body to the physical one. It is usually
attached to the forehead of the physical body and
between the shoulders and bottom of the neck of the
astral body. However, some people see it attached to the
navel of both bodies, while others say it is attached to
the head of both bodies. Eileen Garrett felt it just above
her breasts in her physical body. Just as she was about to
project she would feel "a pull, accompanied by a flutter-
ing, which causes the heart to palpitate, and the breathing to speed up."[3]

Not everyone experiences this. When Dr. Robert Crookall, a leading researcher into the out-of-body experience, began collecting case histories, he found that more than fifty of the first 250 cases he investigated reported seeing this link. However, Celia Green, another researcher who collected many examples in 1966, reported that virtually none of her cases mentioned the silver cord.[4] However, both Yram and Sylvan Muldoon report seeing this cord in their books on the subject.[5] Also, people from all sorts of different cultures have experienced seeing this silver cord. B. J. F. Laubscher, a South African psychiatrist, was told about this silver cord by people in Basuto who could neither read nor write.[6]

Traditional teaching says that if this silver cord breaks, the person will die. In the Bible it says that the person will die if "ever the silver cord be loosed."[7]

Once you are familiar with your surroundings, leave the room. You may find that you have to use the window or door. If they are open you will be able to simply float out of them. You may be able to float through the walls and ceiling as well, but this depends on how solid your astral body is.

If you noticed the silver cord earlier, you will now see that it stretches indefinitely, becoming thinner and thinner the further away you get from your physical body. You will also notice that the strong pull back toward your physical body lessens the further away you move.

Experiment with the three different ways of moving in an astral travel. These were first described by Sylvan Muldoon in *The Projection of the Astral Body*.[8] The first speed is your normal walking speed. Muldoon called the second speed "intermediate speed." This is a fast pace, similar to riding in a car or a fast train. You are aware of the scenery coming towards you and disappearing behind you. The third speed is "supernormal traveling velocity." This occurs when you instantly travel to another place, usually somewhere far away.

As well as these three speeds, there is also levitation, which you have already experienced. This is when you appear to float above your physical body.

Once you have tried walking around your home and traveling at intermediate speed, visualize yourself in your friend's room. This may be inside the house you are in or it may be on the other side of the world. It makes no difference where it is, as the moment you think about it, you will instantly be there. This is the "supernormal traveling velocity" in action.

Take a moment or two to become familiar with the room. See what your friend is doing, assuming he or she is in the room. Float around the room, looking down on it from different positions.

Look for the piece of paper with the numbers written on it. Memorize them. This is not as easy as it sounds. Most people find it difficult to read anything while they are in their astral bodies, so you will need to pay particular attention to the numbers. This is why I suggested a group of numbers, rather than a paragraph or two of writing.

Finally, visualize yourself back in the room where your physical body waits. After familiarizing yourself with the scene, picture yourself back in your physical body and instantly you will be there.

When you feel ready, count from one to five, open your eyes, and stretch. Get up and record everything that happened. In particular, write down the numbers that you looked at in your friend's room.

Do not astral travel again for at least twenty-four hours. You will have a great deal to think about this time. Most importantly, you will know that you can leave the physical body whenever you wish.

When you contact your friend, you will find how good you were at reading and recalling the numbers he or she wrote down. Also find out if your friend was able to tell what time of day or night you visited. Your friend might have been able to see you, or perhaps saw a flash of light, or maybe simply felt your presence. Record anything like this that your friend tells you.

The next time you astral travel, you might want to attempt a different experiment by trying to manipulate something in the physical world. Very few people seem able to do this, but you will not know if you are one of them until you try it yourself. You may try to carry something light from one place to another.

An interesting example of this occurred in 1955 and was reported to the Society for Psychical Research in 1963 by Lucian Landau. His wife, Eileen, frequently astral traveled. One night in 1955, before they were married, Eileen visited Lucian and slept in the spare bedroom. As he was not well at the time, she astral traveled to his room during the night to see how he was. When she told him about it the next morning, Lucian suggested that she do it again that evening but bring a small object with her to leave behind. He suggested his diary and this was placed on a desk in her room.

The next morning Lucian woke at dawn, just in time to see an apparition of Eileen moving slowly backwards in a gliding motion, not walking. He followed her out to the landing, and from this position was able to see both the apparition and Eileen lying asleep in bed. He watched the figure continue to move backwards. When it was halfway between the door and the bed of Eileen's room it disappeared.

Back in his own room, Lucian found a rubber toy dog beside the bed. In the morning, Eileen said that she could not pick up the diary, so she had brought her toy dog instead.[9]

Several people, including myself, witnessed an extraordinary example of someone manipulating the physical world at a private party held a couple of days before a psychic convention in September 1996. The party was held on Hutchinson Island, just off the coast of Florida. One of the people present announced that he was trying to locate a good photograph of Mount Rushmore to use in a brochure he was preparing. Docc Hilford, the host of the party, said that he might be able to find something suitable on the Internet. He turned on his computer and started searching. Riley G, the well-known psychic detective, was at the party and said that he had a photograph of Mount Rushmore in his apartment in New York. Maybe he could astral travel there and bring it back.

The psychics in the room doubted that he could do this, and continued to huddle around the computer. Several minutes later, Riley G quietly announced that he had done it, and that the photograph was now in a cigar box in his hotel room a couple of miles away.

Several people went back to the hotel with Riley. Riley unlocked the door, but did not go in. He pointed at the cigar box lying on the table and asked someone else to open it. Inside was a photograph of Mount Rushmore.

Another interesting example was reported to Celia Green when she was collecting examples of out-of-body experiences in the middle 1960s. A lady was floating down the stairs of her home. As she passed a vase of anemones standing on a sideboard, she reached out with her toes and plucked out a blue flower. She was unable to hold it and it fell to the floor. Seconds later, she was pulled back into her body and went to check. A blue anemone was lying on the floor where she had dropped it during her astral travel.[10]

Choose something light and small when you try this experiment. For instance, you may well be able to turn a page over in a book, but you are unlikely to be able to pick the book up and place it somewhere else.

Even experienced astral travelers can sometimes have difficulty influencing things in the physical world. Keith Harary, also known as Stuart Blue Harary, a well-known astral traveler who was tested extensively by scientists, recorded an experience in which he was floating above his bed and noticed a burning candle in the room. He floated down and tried to blow the candle out. He had to blow on it several times before the flame was extinguished. However, the next morning when he awoke he found that the candle had completely burned down. In his astral body he was unable to put out the flame, even though he thought he had done so.[11]

Yram reported an instance in which he intended to pick up a piece of paper from his chest of drawers and place it on his bed while astral traveling. Once he was out of his body, he noticed two pieces of paper on his chest of drawers. He placed them both on the bed. When he returned to his body, he found that the paper had not moved at all, even though he was certain he had successfully moved it. He tried again and blew the piece of paper. It moved. He then examined his hands and arms and found them to be solid, but once he was back in his physical body he found that he had not moved the paper at all.[12] This shows how difficult working in the astral realms can be, even for highly experienced practitioners.

During your first out-of-body experiences, explore as much of the world around you as you can. Visit places that you enjoyed visiting in the past. Visit friends and neighbors and see if you can make them aware of your presence.

You may find that you are as successful as a lady acquaintance of William T. Stead. She thoroughly enjoyed leaving her body and astrally visiting friends who lived far away. For a while she caused her friends great worry when she suddenly materialized in front of them, as they thought that she had died. However, these occurrences gradually became less worrisome as her friends got used to them and looked forward to her unexpected visits.[13]

You can instantly visit any place you want by simply thinking about it. In the early stages of your development as an astral traveler, you will find it easier to travel to places that you have already visited in your physical body than places you have not seen. This is because you can easily visualize places you have visited. If you want to visit somewhere you have never been, try to familiarize yourself with the location by reading about it and looking at photographs. That way you will be able to visualize it more easily.

There is no need to fly along the same route you would take if you were visiting the place in your physical body. It is easy to get disoriented and frustrated if you do this, as everything looks different when you are flying in your astral body.

Some people say that they are aware of a blurred impression of flying from place to place.[14] This means that they are using Sylvan Muldoon's "intermediate speed" of movement. Although you can certainly travel in this way, it is easier to use "supernormal traveling velocity" when traveling long distances, so that you are instantly where you want to be.

To travel long distances you need to have a strong desire to go there. As you will know by now, there is a strong pull back towards your physical body while you are astral traveling. Consequently, if the desire is not strong enough, you will not be able to visit that particular place.

Keep accurate records of everything you do, and allow plenty of time between your astral travels. This will become less important as you gain experience and confidence in the astral plane.

You will experience occasional shocks, but nothing anywhere near as frightening as was intimated in the books that appeared in the first half of the twentieth century.[15] From time to time you will suddenly find yourself forced back into your physical body when you least expect it. This can be jarring and shocking. When this occurs, simply lie quietly until your breathing returns to normal. You might find it helpful to stretch, then relax for a couple of minutes to allow your astral body to return comfortably into position.

These sudden returns to the body are caused by one of two reasons: either you happened to think about your physical body while traveling, or the body needed you back to handle some situation. It is annoying to find yourself back in your body when you are in the middle of doing something exciting, but it is part of the process and something you gradually become used to. Naturally, it is a good thing that the physical body summons you back if it needs you for any reason.

If you encounter something frightening on the astral plane, all you need do is think of returning to the body, and you will instantly be there. On those occasions I do not think about returning to the room where my body is, but return directly to my physical body.

Once you have explored the world around you thoroughly and convinced yourself of the safety and sheer pleasure of astral flight, you are ready to move on to more advanced astral traveling. We will start on that in the next chapter.

Chapter Eight

Exploring Different Worlds

NOW THAT YOU FEEL RELAXED AND CONFIDENT WHILE astral traveling, the time has come to investigate different worlds.

Think about a time in history that has always fascinated you. I love Monteverdi's madrigals, so I chose late sixteenth-century Italy for one of my first astral travels into the past. In fact, I even chose a certain place and particular day because I wanted to attend the first performance of his opera *Orfeo*. I have since returned to that period of time on many occasions to experience and learn more.

Since I am interested in history, I would be happy to go almost anywhere, but there needs to be a purpose for the trip, so think carefully about exactly where you would like to visit. There is no point in visiting Scandinavia in 1600 if you really wanted to be in London that year attending the first performance of Hamlet. Think carefully about where you want to go and why you want to be there.

Once you are out of your body, simply tell yourself where you want to be and you will instantly be transported back through time and space to the period you wished to see.

When you get there, see what clothes you are wearing. Usually, you will be wearing the correct clothing of the period, but if not, simply request it and you will immediately be in the correct attire.

There is no danger in moving through time in this way. You can instantly return to your physical body whenever you wish. In fact, most of the time, you will find yourself back in your body sooner than you wanted to be.

Are there things you would have liked to have said to friends or relatives who are no longer alive? Go back through time just a few years, so that you can see them again and tell them how much you love them. I know myself just how valuable this can be from a healing point of view.

It is also possible to see deceased relatives and friends on the astral plane. Instead of seeing them in the physical world, you can have a lengthy conversation with them in the astral world. You can learn a great deal this way.

You can also request conversations from interesting people in the past. Would you like to speak with Christopher Columbus? Simply request a conversation once you are out of your physical body, and most of the time, your request will be honored. I find it interesting that on the astral plane you can speak freely with people from any time and any culture, and they will be able to understand you and respond in your language. The problems created by people speaking different languages do not apply on the astral plane.

Maybe you would like to travel into the future. Simply name a place and date and you will immediately be there. If you carefully observe what you see and hear, you will be able to bring that information back into your present physical incarnation and be considered a prophet.

Do you want to know what your life will be like five or ten years from now? Move forward that amount of time and see. If you are not happy with what you see as your personal future, ask what changes you need to put into place to alter your future life. We are all capable of achieving much more than we actually do, but the problem is that we do not always know what we need to change. From your vantage point in the future, you will be able to use hindsight ahead of time and create the sort of future that you really want.

How about visiting other planets to see what they are like? It is just as easy. Simply request it once you are out of your body and you will be there. Think how long that silver cord will be when you are exploring Mars!

Everyone experiences things differently when they astral travel. My experiences will not be the same as yours. This is as it should be, of course. Even in the physical world, no two people see things in exactly the same way. You and I may both look at the same incident in the physical world and give two completely different accounts of it to a third person.

Some people experience "helpers" when they astral travel. Helpers are people who gently look after the person while he or she is out of the body. However, I have never seen them. Maybe they are there and I have been unable to see them, or perhaps the people who do see them are experiencing their astral travel in a different way than I do.

Even the people who have "helpers" see them in different ways. One lady told me that her helpers were always nuns, dressed in full habit. Another saw angels, while a third was always accompanied by an elderly man with a "long, sad face." Yram saw and heard a variety of different types of helpers, but they were usually in the shape of dogs.[1] Yram thought that the guides or helpers rarely showed their faces, but sent an image of something that inspires confidence, such as a dog. Robert Monroe, in his book *Journeys Out of the Body*, says that he does not always see his helpers but can usually feel or sense them. On one trip "the feeling of gentle but firm hands on each side of me was very strong."[2] On another occasion the helper was "a rich, deep voice—yet not a voice."[3]

Robert Monroe was also able to see demons, spirits, and a variety of humanoid-like entities in his astral travels to strange and fantastic worlds. Some of these attacked him or attached themselves to his body. I have never experienced anything remotely like this in my travels. In his book *Practical Astral Projection*, Yram wrote: "A thought is often enough to cause an entity which pleases or displeases us to appear or disappear."[4] Later in the same book he wrote: "As the majority of people are ignorant of the possibility of living consciously in space, they surround themselves with imaginary creations.... Imagination is a reality."[5] Robert Monroe eventually realized that nothing could hurt him while he was out of his body, and that it was purely his own fear that held him back. Once he discovered this, his fears vanished and he stopped worrying about his well-being while astral traveling. However, his experiences show that when we are astral traveling we can create entire worlds inside our imagination, but they will seem incredibly real.

It certainly seems that there are two distinct types of astral travel. One explores a world that is identical in every way to the world we live in, but the other examines a more mystical world with all sorts of different realities.

Some people explain astral travels as visits to parallel worlds, where everything is the same as in our physical world but different at the same time. An interesting example of this occurred to Oliver Fox on one of his first astral travels. He was standing on the sidewalk outside his home and could see everything as usual. He was about to walk into his home when he suddenly noticed that the small, bluish-gray rectangular stones that made up the pavement had turned around ninety degrees. Normally, their short sides abutted the curb, but in his astral travel the long sides were now parallel to the curb.[6]

For most people, this parallel world is similar in most respects to the world we live in every day, but some people, such as Robert Monroe, are able to travel to worlds that are different from our physical world in every possible way. This is because the astral plane has been called "the realm of visual imagination"[7] and consists of a number of levels, or subplanes. It is possible to visit any of the levels. However, most people have no desire to do this and are content to explore a parallel world to our own one.

I am frequently asked about love in the astral world. Yes, it certainly is possible and occurs in many forms.

If you have had a strong relationship with someone who has died, you can continue that relationship by visiting that person on the "other side." Many people have reported instances of astral sex, so it is possible to carry on a full relationship with a deceased loved one. However, astral sex is not the same as physical sex. There is an exchange of energy and a feeling of ecstasy, but although it is satisfying, it is still different than sex on the physical plane.

In fact, sex between humans and spirit entities has been part of the mythology of many races since the beginning of time. Instances can be seen in Greek, Roman, Norse, and Celtic mythology. Geoffrey of Monmouth wrote that Merlin was the result of a union between the Princess of Demetia and an incubus.[8] In Mexico there are women considered to be witches who use an unguent called *toloachi* to help them contact their spirit lovers.[9] Toloachi is made up of a number of deadly, poisonous herbs. There is certainly no need to use anything like this to make contact with your astral lover.

It is possible to continue a relationship when you are separated for some reason. A man I know travels regularly on business trips. Before he leaves he arranges times to meet his partner on the astral plane, so that their relationship can continue to develop and grow even while they are apart.

If you do not have a partner in the physical world, you can, if you wish, find one in the astral. Be careful, though. Just as in the physical world, you need to be cautious and selective. Take your time. If you are seeking a good relationship, you will find one, but you may need to be patient until that special person arrives. You will find that, once you start astral traveling frequently, the astral world can often be a lonely place, and you will not be able to converse with many people on the astral plane. Consequently, you need to be especially careful and not fall head over heels in love with the first person you come across in the astral world. Even when you find your special person, insist on a period of time to get to know each other. If you want this relationship to last, it has to be based on much more than sex.

Many people believe that such an astral lover is someone you have already known and loved in previous incarnations. Consequently, you will find it easy to recognize this person as soon as you find him or her. You will be able to astral travel together to places that were important to you both in previous lifetimes, and you will be able to travel into the future to look at the lives you will be spending together there.

There are many advantages to this sort of relationship. Astral sex is safe. Unlike the physical world, you do not need to meet and spend time with the person's family and friends. An astral lover will provide security, fulfillment, and companionship. Interestingly, this relationship will also make it easier for you to attract a partner in the physical world. This is because you will be less anxious, and any feelings of desperation will disappear. You will be calm and serene, and consequently be more likely to attract people to you. Also, your astral lover will want you to have a stable, loving relationship in the physical world because he or she will have your happiness and well-being at heart.

The astral worlds are fascinating places to visit and explore. Your knowledge and understanding will grow enormously. You will change as a person and grow inwardly. Other people are likely to comment about this and not be able to say exactly what changes have taken place. It is up to you to decide whether or not to tell them what you are doing.

Chapter Nine

Other Methods of Astral Traveling

I HAVE ALREADY EXPLAINED THE METHOD THAT I, AND most of my students, have found to be the easiest way of leaving the body. However, everyone is different and, because of this, the method I personally prefer for leaving the body may not be the best method for you.

I have successfully astral traveled using all of the methods described in this chapter. I have left out at least as many methods that have not worked for me. Presumably they work for other people, but because I could not achieve success with them, I have not included them here. I remember spending months trying to astral travel using a method described by Oliver Fox in his book *Astral Projection*. This method involved sending the body to sleep while the mind remains awake.[1] This may sound similar to the progressive relaxation method, but is not, because his method involves muscular rigidity and a degree of pain. I found this impossible to achieve, so have not included it.

I have also left out all the different methods that involve drugs. Certainly, for thousands of years people in various cultures have utilized hallucinogens to help them leave their bodies, and I have spoken to several people who involuntarily astral traveled while they were under the influence of drugs. However, drugs are not necessary and can sometimes produce frightening experiences. They are also inclined to distort the way the person sees things and do not give a true picture of what should be a wonderful experience.

Meditation Method

It may sound surprising that you can astral travel while meditating, but in fact this is one of the easier ways of leaving the body, as it is smooth and effortless. In fact, there have been many reports of people who spontaneously astral traveled while meditating. Some of the older methods of leaving the body need fierce determination and hard work, but meditation needs neither.

All you do is sit back in a comfortable chair, close your eyes, relax, and think pleasant thoughts. After a few minutes of this, progressively relax all of the muscles of your body, until you feel as limp and relaxed as a rag doll.

You are now physically relaxed. The next step is to quiet your mind and allow your consciousness to be still and empty. You may feel some strange sensations as you do this. You may feel a cooling breeze, for instance. I sometimes experience a gentle, not unpleasant, humming sound in my ears. Shapes and forms may appear in your consciousness. Look at them, but do not let them start your thinking processes again.

Once your physical body and conscious mind are both totally relaxed, lie still and wait. You may find your head appears to grow larger. You may find that you are moving. This could be a gentle rocking from side to side, or it could be a powerful vibration. The vibration may feel like uncontrolled shivering or a shudder that won't stop. It is difficult to allow these things to occur without thinking about them. However, it is vital that you do not think, as these signs mean that your consciousness is about to leave your physical body.

Suddenly, and it will happen in just an instant, you will be free of your body. You will probably find yourself hovering just a few feet above your physical body.

Now, think about where you want to go or where you would like to be. Simply fantasize and imagine it in your mind. Do not analyze what you are thinking or seeing. Simply flow with them and see where they take you.

You may visit someone who is or was special to you. You may visit a famous teacher from the past. You could well visit a place that you have always wanted to visit. You may see yourself as you are now, or perhaps older or younger than you are now. It can be a fascinating, and highly rewarding, experience to have a three-way conversation with yourself, perhaps with the other "yous" being twenty years younger and twenty years older than you are right now.

Observe everything as clearly as you can. Do not think too much about the actual experience as you are living it. You can evaluate the experience afterwards.

When you feel ready, tell yourself to return to your physical body. Pause for a minute or two before counting up to five and opening your eyes. Think about what you have done. This method can sometimes be deceptive. Did it feel like mind travel or was it an astral travel? Did you see everything in brilliant color? Were you able to communicate clearly with people you met on the trip? Did you see, smell, taste, and feel at least as vividly as you do while in your physical body? If so, you successfully astral traveled.

If you are not sure, repeat the meditation method several times. Like everything else, practice makes perfect. One day, you will be doing the meditation method and suddenly become aware that you are astral traveling. The surprise of this realization will probably bring you straight back to the present, but from then on you will have no doubts as to the veracity of this method.

There are many methods of meditation, and if you are familiar with another technique of meditation, such as gazing at a candle flame or repeating a mantra, you should continue to use this method, but with the ultimate aim of using it as a springboard to an out-of-body experience.

Swing Method

This method is a particularly pleasant one that I use frequently. You start in the usual way with a progressive relaxation. When the physical body is completely relaxed, imagine that you are on a swing, swinging to and fro in an arc from the tip of your nose to the top of your head. Concentrate on the tip of your nose and the top of your head, but feel your whole body as if it were on a playground swing. As with a normal swing, try to swing just a little bit higher each time. Higher and higher, higher and higher, until you feel that the swing will make a complete revolution. At the highest point of the arc, just before you feel it will keep on going in a complete circle, let go in your mind, and you will suddenly find yourself outside your body. It is a strange sensation, as you will feel in your stomach that you have been swinging, but will also be able to see your physical body relaxed and motionless where you left it.

Once you have done this a few times you will find that you do not need to go through the progressive relaxation procedure first. You will be able to sit down quietly somewhere, close your eyes, and visualize yourself swinging higher and higher until you suddenly detach yourself from your physical body.

The French Method

This method was used extensively by leading French pioneers of astral travel in the late nineteenth century. At this time, the French were far ahead of the rest of the world in researching out-of-body experiences, and they recorded a large number of impressive successes.

One well-known, humorous example concerned a young man who was hypnotized and then asked to leave his physical body to see what his father was doing. In his astral body, the young man saw his father walking across town and into a house of dubious repute. This proved to be exactly what the father was doing at the time, and he pleaded with the experimenter to never, ever perform such an experiment again![2]

Two of these French pioneers published a great deal of valuable information. The first of these was Hector Durville, secretary of the Magnetic Society in France and a keen hypnotist. He was a dedicated researcher who spent much of his life attempting to prove the existence of the etheric double or astral body. Starting in 1908, he published a large number of detailed reports about his discoveries.

Arguably, Durville's greatest discovery was that people who showed no interest or knowledge about the psychic world were often surprisingly good at determining when an invisible presence (astral traveler) was in the room.

"When the phantom approaches the spectators," Durville wrote in 1908, "nine out of ten of them become aware of its presence by a feeling of coolness which comes over them and which disappears soon after it has gone away again. Some perceive distinctly a sort of breath, which somewhat resembles that felt when standing near an electrostatic machine in operation."[3]

Hector Durville believed that hypnosis was necessary to achieve an astral projection. His contemporary, Dr. Charles Lancelin, a physician and keen psychical researcher, thought that it should be possible to achieve an out-of-body experience without the need of a hypnotist. In 1908, Lancelin produced *Methodes de Dédoublement Personnel*, a 559-page book on his research and findings.

Lancelin believed that to successfully astral travel you needed three qualities. The first was good health, the second a "nervous temperament," and the third a strong conscious and unconscious will to leave the physical body. By "nervous temperament" Lancelin meant someone who was easily hypnotizable. The "conscious and unconscious will" means that the person must desire to astral travel so much that the will becomes an unconscious motivating factor, as well as a conscious force.

The process is simple, but it takes most people several attempts before they can do it successfully. I think this is because it is not easy to achieve a state of both conscious and unconscious willing. Consequently, it would be beneficial to think about leaving the physical body whenever possible for a week or so before first trying this method. Tell yourself how important it is for you to learn this skill and that you will benefit enormously from being able to do it.

When you are ready to begin, choose a quiet, still evening and, as always, make sure that you will not be disturbed. The room should be dark and reasonably warm. You should also be alone.

Close your eyes and become aware of your breathing. Then bring your attention to the toes of one foot. Focus on those toes to the exclusion of everything else. Feel the astral double detaching itself from your physical body at this point.

Once you have achieved this, do the same with the toes of the other foot. Then focus on a small portion of the sole of one foot and feel the astral body detaching there as well. Carry on up through your entire body, feeling the astral body detaching at every point, until you reach the top of your head. Detach the astral body from here as well, so that the astral body is now lying loosely around you.

Focus on your forehead and will the astral body to leave. This is where the conscious and unconscious willing really comes into play. Will it to leave with every fiber of your being, and you will find that suddenly you are looking down on yourself from up near the ceiling.

Dr. Lancelin believed that leaving the body was something that should be approached slowly and carefully. It was rare for anyone in his experience to be able to astral travel immediately on the first attempt. It took time, patience, and, of course, a great deal of conscious and unconscious will.

The Whirlwind Method

The Whirlwind method was one frequently used by the French occultist Yram around the time of World War I. Quite coincidentally, at the same time in the United States, Prescott Hall, a member of the American Society for Psychical Research, was also astral traveling in the same way. He published his experiences in the *Journal of the American Society for Psychical Research* in 1916.[4]

Interestingly enough, Yram seemed to have discovered this method by himself, but Prescott Hall received it as a series of spirit messages that came through Minnie Keeler, a Spiritualist medium.

In 1902, two friends told Prescott Hall about their astral travels. At this time, Hall was rather skeptical about psychic matters, but he visited a medium to see if she could provide any information on the subject. Nothing came of this, but several years later, in 1909, Hall contacted Minnie Keeler to see if she could contact a deceased friend for him. In his articles about this subject Prescott Hall refers to his dead friend, rather mysteriously, as Miss X. Contact was made and over a period of time many messages came through. Several of them contained information about astral travel.

This gave Prescott Hall an interesting idea. If Miss X would be able to give him an effective method of astral traveling that had not been previously published, it would be a wonderful way of proving the veracity of spirit communication. At the next sitting, Prescott Hall asked Miss X if this would be possible. Miss X was as intrigued with the idea as Hall was, and put him in touch with several deceased Oriental masters who began communicating vast amounts of information through Minnie Keeler. Prescott Hall received information on a weekly basis from 1909 to 1915, totalling some 350 pages in all. This material included not only instructions on how to astral travel, but also lengthy lectures on the nature of spiritual life, the astral body, the human soul, and life after death.

The material was so detailed and exhaustive in content that Professor James Hyslop, then president of the American Society for Psychical Research and editor of their *Journal*, conducted an inquiry into Minnie Keeler's background to see if she could have learned the information is some other way. As it turned out, her study on the subject was negligible and consisted of casual reading of a few books and magazines. Mrs. Keeler was not a professional medium and showed little interest in the material that came through. Dr. Crookall referred to these "communications" as being received "by Hall (who was quite skeptical about the matter) through the mediumship of Mrs. Keeler (who had no interest in it)."[5]

All the same, several of the methods that came through Minnie Keeler for inducing out-of-body experiences have been referred to with great respect by such later authorities as Sylvan Muldoon and Hereward Carrington.

Unfortunately, Prescott Hall did not organize and record his material well. In 1964, Dr. Robert Crookall published *The Techniques of Astral Projection*, which evaluated and rewrote the original material.

The method consists of two parts. The first relates to diet, and specific instructions were given.

1. The student should avoid meat. Fasting may be useful for some people, but everyone should cut down on the amount of food they eat.

2. The student should not eat at all for an hour or two before any astral travels.

3. The student should eat mainly fruit and vegetables. Carrots are believed to be especially beneficial.

4. Raw eggs are considered favorable and aid astral traveling.

5. Nuts, especially peanuts, are considered bad and should not be consumed while the student is training.

6. All liquids are beneficial, but none should be drunk to excess. Coffee and alcohol should be avoided on any day when astral travel is attempted.

7. Tobacco and other drugs should be avoided. "Tobacco draws noxious influences and puts undesirable products into the blood stream, but its chief evil is that it interferes with good spirits and interferes with their approach."[6]

8. The good news comes at the end: "After five or six months of development...advanced persons can eat anything."[7]

The specific length of time required of this diet before starting to astral travel is not given, though you should keep to it for at least two weeks before starting to astral travel.

When you are ready to travel, you should make yourself comfortable in a warm and darkened room. You need to "sit sufficiently erect so that the circulation is not interfered with, for blood pressure is an important factor."[8] The arms and legs should be uncrossed.

It is recommended that you have a dish of water nearby. This is the method of protection that the spirits suggested to Prescott Hall through Minnie Keeler. Alternative suggestions were "putting one's hands in water" or using "the vapor of water."[9] I think a glass of water is more practical and convenient, and washing one's hands before starting is a good idea.

The student should then concentrate on taking deep breaths and relaxing. "Breathing is important, as the pulse in the brain is synchronous with it. Therefore various breathing exercises (are of great help) . . . . For getting out of the body, *holding the breath* is of value, but holding it out has no effect."[10] Once you are sufficiently relaxed and breathing steadily, visualize one of the following scenarios:

1. Imagine yourself inside a large cone. Squeeze yourself into the very top and then pop your way out.

2. Visualize a whirlpool and see yourself swirling in it. As you approach the vortex see yourself becoming a small dot, which expands as you emerge out of it. After going around several times, see yourself swirling through the vortex and out of your body.

3. This is similar to the last one. See yourself body-surfing on a large wave. As the wave curls downward, see yourself go with it and out of your body.

4. Visualize yourself clinging to the center of a large coil of rope. As it is pulled out see yourself being drawn out of your body at the same time.

5. Visualize yourself floating in a tank of water that is slowly being filled. As it fills up you find a small hole in the side, and you leave your body as you squeeze through it.

6. Visualize yourself gazing at yourself through a mirror. As you stare steadily at your reflection, visualize your consciousness moving into the image you see.

7. Visualize yourself sitting on a large, steaming, limp cloth. See yourself gradually becoming the steam and leaving your physical body as the steam rises.

All of these images are pleasant to visualize, and it is helpful to have something different to use every time you go through the procedure. They have the advantage of being simple to picture, and allow you to focus the mind on something away from the physical body.

Two years later, Prescott Hall wrote another report.[11] In this he described his own experiments with the different visualizations and added several more. Unfortunately, none of them are as easy to visualize as the earlier ones. The only two that I have had success with are:

1. Visualize yourself flying through the air to the Himalayas. See the landscape changing beneath you, feel the pressure of the air as you fly through space, and, when you feel ready, simply fly out of your physical body.

2. Visualize yourself as a large soap bubble floating through space. See yourself passing different planets as you drift through the galaxy. When you feel ready, pop the bubble and leave your physical body behind.

I mentioned that Yram was using a similar method in France at the same time as Prescott Hall was receiving his "channeled" information. In his book *Practical Astral Projection*, Yram describes being sucked up by a whirlwind. Although he described the process as painless, he always remained on the defensive as he never knew where the whirlwind was going to deposit his astral body. He tried to influence himself to astral project into his own room before exploring other places, but at times, the whirlwind would ignore this and he would find himself carried "away in an etheric 'draught' which is extraordinarily interesting to experience."[12] Yram experienced a feeling of great speed and was temporarily deafened by the "howling tempest." Generally, he had no control over his movements and could be transported standing up, lying on his stomach, head or feet first, or even sitting down as if in a chair.

However, he always found that astral traveling in this way refreshed and revitalized him, even though other methods left him feeling exhausted.

The Visualization Technique (1)

Many people learn how to astral travel by vividly visualizing themselves doing it in their minds before doing it in reality. If you find it easy to picture things in your mind, you will find this a highly effective way of leaving the body.

To start with, you will have to test your visualization abilities. Sit down quietly where you will not be disturbed and close your eyes. Start by picturing a scene from your early childhood, preferably when you were younger than five years old. See the scene as clearly as you can. Picture the surroundings and anyone else who was there with you. Become aware of any sounds, smells, feelings or other sensations that are connected with this scene. Once you have made this image as clear as you can, let it go and briefly picture a blank screen.

On this screen, visualize the front door of your home. Again see it as clearly as you can. Notice any marks or scratches on the surface. Become aware of the door-frame, the keyhole, and anything else you can recall about this door. Again, once you have seen this as vividly as you can, let it go and picture the blank screen again.

On the blank screen, visualize your bedroom. See it as clearly as possible. Notice the bed, any other furniture, the carpets, drapes, windows, and door. See it so clearly that you can even see any specks of dust that may be present. See what's on top of the wardrobe, and the positions of any clothes, shoes, or other articles that might be lying on the floor, bed, or chair.

Once you have seen this as vividly as you can, let it go until the screen is blank again. For the final visualization exercise, see yourself walking across the surface of the Moon. See it as clearly as you can. Notice how you feel as you walk along. Become aware of any sounds you may hear. Totally immerse yourself in the experience.

Once you have pictured this scene as vividly as you can, let it go and open your eyes. Which of those experiences did you "see" most clearly? There is no right or wrong answer, though most people see either the early childhood scene or the Moon experience more clearly than the two things they have probably already seen at least once today.

Were all four scenes clear to you, or were one or two easier to visualize? Were you more aware of the sounds, smells, and feelings than the pictures?

You may want to have a fresh look at your front door and bedroom to see how accurately you pictured them. Do not be concerned if you "saw" clothes stacked on the bed when there are none today. You may have been "see-ing" the bedroom as it was yesterday, rather than the way it is right now. One man I knew saw his front door with exceptional clarity, but discovered when he went to look at the door that he had "seen" the door of his childhood home rather than the door of the house he lives in now.

Everyone is different. I have had people who saw all four scenes so clearly that they felt as if they were living them, but I have also had people who could not "see" any of them. Most people come somewhere in the mid-dle. They can picture the scenes, but in different degrees of clarity.

If you were unable to see any of the scenes clearly, you will find little point in trying this method. However, this will prove an excellent method for you if you were able to see everything. If you come somewhere in the middle, though, you should try one more test before proceeding.

You will need to find a completely blank wall. You may find that you need to hang up a sheet to get a blank surface like a movie screen. In front of this place a pot-ted plant or ornament. Sit several feet away from the object and stare at it for four or five minutes. Then close your eyes and visualize the object you were staring at. See it as clearly and as perfectly as possible.

Keep your mind focused on this visualization for sev-eral minutes. If the object fades away in your mind, open your eyes and look at it again.

Once you can do this successfully you can progress to the next stage. Place an upturned glass or cup on a table and sit several feet away from it. Close your eyes and visualize your conscious mind inside the upturned object. This sounds more difficult than it is. With your eyes closed simply focus your entire attention on the upturned object. After the visualization exercises this will prove surprisingly easy. After a while you will notice that the only things you are aware of are the object and your conscious mind. With practice, these two will merge into one, and you will have achieved your aim.

Now that you have achieved this, you can practice sending your conscious mind anywhere you wish. You will find that you can look at yourself from wherever your consciousness is placed, and will ultimately be able to think from that position as well.

Once this is mastered, you can progress to using these skills to astral travel.

Sit down quietly, close your eyes, and take several deep breaths. Become very aware of your breathing, slowly counting as you inhale, hold the breath, and then exhale. You should hold your breath for at least as long as the time it took to inhale, and then exhale slowly.

Visualize yourself in your mind's eye, and then gradually visualize your astral body slowly rising up and away from the physical body. Once it is free, you can astral travel with it to anywhere you want to go. When you are ready to return, all you need do is visualize the astral body entering the physical body and you will instantly be back in your physical body.

Aleister Crowley taught a variation of the visualization method to his students. Each student was to visualize a door in a large blank wall. A special symbol that related to the student was engraved on the door. The student would watch the door slowly opening and visualize him or herself walking through it. After practicing this for some time, the student would suddenly find him or herself astral traveling.

One criticism of the visualization method is that the whole experience could be a visualization rather than reality. In fact, this could well be the case initially. It is a little bit like learning to fly using a simulator. You learn how to do it in a safe, supportive environment, and then, when you are ready, you are put into a real plane and know exactly what to do. Of course, when you are using the visualization technique there is no way of knowing when you are ready. However, by going through the procedure a number of times, you will become better and better at doing it and ultimately will find yourself free of the body.

The Visualization Technique (2)

This method starts off in exactly the same way as the previous Visualization Technique. Practice visualizing the four scenes until you can see at least two of them clearly in your mind.

Once you can do that quickly and easily, lie flat on your back on the floor with your eyes closed. You can use a cushion or pillow to support your head if necessary. Make sure that you are wearing loose-fitting clothes and that the room is reasonably warm.

With your eyes closed, picture a duplicate of yourself floating in space two or three feet above you. This duplicate is perfect in every way. He or she is wearing the same clothes that you are wearing and looks completely real. As you visualize this image in your mind, you will gradually find that it becomes more and more solid and real.

Ask yourself, "Which one is me?" and you will experience a brief moment of uncertainty until you realize that, naturally, the "you" who is lying on the floor is the real "you."

Ask yourself, "What if the floating me was the real me?" For a moment or two, the same doubt will cross your mind.

Pause for a few moments, picturing your double, and then see if you can will your consciousness into the image of yourself. When it happens, it will occur suddenly and you'll experience a moment or two of uncertainty again. It is important at this stage to remain calm and relaxed, as otherwise your consciousness will immediately return to your physical body.

Once you are comfortable with your consciousness in its temporary home, you can start looking down on yourself in a reversal of the way you began the exercise.

When you are ready you can move wherever you wish.

Willpower Method

Like the Visualization Method, the Willpower Method is not for everyone. In my work as a hypnotherapist, people constantly tell me that they have no willpower. This is not true in the majority of cases. Most people find it hard to change a habit or addiction using willpower alone. This is because our emotions are much more powerful than our will, and consequently win every time. If people who are trying to lose weight are feeling depressed, stressed, or bored and then have a plate of tempting food put in front of them, will they be able to refuse? Probably not, as food can cheer people up, even though the whole time they are eating they are aware that they should not be doing it.

However, practicing the Willpower Method is a useful exercise and I know many people who have amazed themselves by succeeding in leaving their bodies with this method, after having difficulty with other techniques.

Sit down in a comfortable armchair. Make sure that your lower back is supported. As usual, the room should be warm, dark or semi-dark, and with the phone disconnected. Place the backs of your hands on your thighs, so the palms are facing upwards.

Take several deep breaths, until your breathing becomes slow and rhythmical and you do not need to concentrate on it.

Start thinking of your need to astral travel. Think of your purpose in making this particular trip. Remain quietly confident that you will be able to leave the body.

Now it is time to use your willpower. Silently say to yourself, "I will leave my body. I am ready to leave my body. My astral body is ready to leave. I want to leave NOW!"

Wait several seconds and then repeat it again. Do this perhaps a dozen times, repeating the words like a mantra.

You may find that your body starts to vibrate and then you are suddenly free of the body and looking down on your physical body. If so, carry on with your exploration. If you do not succeed after repeating the mantra a dozen times, open your eyes and go for a brisk walk.

Think positive thoughts while on your walk. Do not think that you have failed. In fact, you have not. You have actually moved one step closer to success. After your walk, repeat the process again. A good, brisk walk will have put oxygen into your brain and you are more likely to succeed on the second attempt. If success still eludes you, simply congratulate yourself on getting closer to leaving the physical body and try again the following day.

Chakra Method

The ancient Eastern yogis believed that we all have seven energy centers, or chakras, in our bodies (Figure 5, page 123). It is possible to develop these centers by meditation and study, and thus achieve a better, fuller, more spiritual life.

The seven chakras are revolving circles of energy, and in fact the word *chakra* comes from a Sanskrit word that means "wheel." They are found inside the aura located parallel to the spine in the principal nadi, or channel.

When each chakra is activated in sequence, in a form of chakra meditation, your consciousness is raised by the increase of psychic energy. Once this process is complete, it is a simple matter to move the consciousness out of the body and to astral travel.

Naturally, this method is easier for people who have studied the chakras.[13] However, this is a useful variation of the meditation methods and you may wish to try it even if you have not previously read much about the chakras.

The root chakra is located at the base of the spine at the perineum. It gives feelings of being grounded to the earth. At its most basic, it represents the survival instinct.

The sacral chakra is at the level of the sacrum. It looks after the fluid functions of the body and our sex drive. It is also related to our sense of taste.

The solar chakra is located in the solar plexus and provides feelings of expansiveness and well-being. It is also related to our sense of sight.

The heart chakra is located by the heart. It relates to our sense of touch and feelings such as tenderness and sympathy.

The throat chakra is located at the base of the throat and is related to the sense of sound.

The brow chakra is found between the eyebrows and relates to the power of thought and creativity. For anything to be created, someone has to think first. This makes the brow chakra a potent force.

The crown chakra is located at the top of the head, near the pineal gland in the brain. It relates to enlightenment. There is a growing body of evidence that indicates that the pineal gland is responsible for many psychic activities, including astral travel. Dr. Serena Roney Dougal discovered that a certain hallucinogen that is used in many parts of South America for clairvoyance and divination purposes was almost identical to a chemical that is produced by the pineal gland. This chemical produces an altered state of consciousness that makes us more receptive to psychic occurrences.[14]

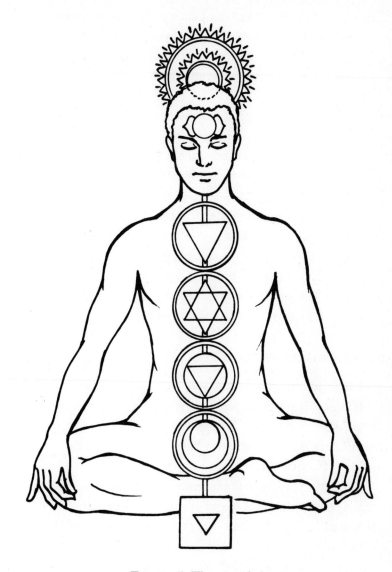

FIGURE 5. *The seven chakras.*

This is what makes the Chakra Method so effective. Each chakra gathers energy and power as you meditate on it, and this compounds as you gradually move up the body to the crown chakra, and from there into an astral projection.

The methodology is exactly the same as in meditation. You need to sit down quietly somewhere, close your eyes, and concentrate on the root chakra. Visualize it as a swirling ball of energy that gains power with every revolution. Taking your time, move up to the sacral chakra and then on through the body until each chakra is alive and active.

When you can feel each chakra's energy, individually and collectively, and visualize them all in your mind, you will suddenly find your consciousness outside your body.

A full chakra meditation is provided in the Appendix.

Affirmation Method

I have found that this method works extremely well for people who use affirmations to help them in different areas of their lives. It does not seem to be nearly as effective with people who have not already discovered how effective affirmations can be.

An affirmation is simply a short phrase or sentence that the person repeats over and over again, like a mantra. The first real affirmation was "Every day and in every way, I am becoming better and better." This was used and popularized by Emil Coué (1857–1926) in the early 1900s. He was able to help many people with it and, when he arrived in the United States to lecture on his findings, thousands of people came down to the wharves to see him.

Repetition of an affirmation helps it to sink deeper and deeper into our subconscious minds, and in time we simply act on it as if it were true. In fact, belief is not necessary. You may, for instance, say to yourself, "I am rich and prosperous" at a time when you are in desperate financial straits. You will know that this affirmation is not true at the present time, but your subconscious mind does not know that, and will act on it and make it a reality.

You can create affirmations for just about anything. If you have been meaning to clean up your garden shed for several months, but have not quite got around to it, you can say an affirmation until the job gets done. You might say, "I am cleaning up the shed" twenty or thirty times a day. Notice that affirmations are always said in the present tense. You do not say, "I will clean up the garden shed," as that could occur tomorrow or in ten years.

Naturally, it might still take time before your garden shed gets cleaned, but you are instilling the thought in your brain and, one day, you will suddenly get busy and do it.

More useful affirmations might be, "I am happy" or "I am well." If you want to attract more money, say, "I am wealthy. I have all the money I need." You will know, as you say this that this might not be true, but your inner mind does not know that and will set about providing you with whatever you think about.

You can also use affirmations to help you leave the body. As you go about your day, simply say to yourself as many times as you can, "I am going to astral travel. I am going to leave my body." It would help to say these words out loud when you can, but repeating them over and over silently to yourself is almost as effective.

In the evening, you can sit down comfortably somewhere in the normal manner, close your eyes, and go through a progressive relaxation exercise.

When you feel that you are totally relaxed, simply say the following affirmation silently to yourself: "I am ready to astral travel. I am ready to leave my body. I am going to astral travel. I am going to leave my body."

Keep on repeating these words silently to yourself over and over again.

What you have done is create a readiness and an expectation of astral travel. It might not happen on the first few times you try this, but ultimately, you will find your whole body starting to vibrate and you suddenly will be free and out of your physical body.

It is also useful to say this affirmation as many times as possible throughout the day, even when you are trying other methods, as your inner mind will lock on to the thought and make it happen.

The Christos Method

I will never forget the feeling of exhilaration and excitement I felt after first reading *Windows of the Mind: The Christos Experience* by the Australian writer G. M. Glaskin. This feeling was compounded even more when I tried the simple techniques with a couple of friends and found that they worked. What particularly amazed me was that the technique worked even with people who were skeptical about the whole subject.

The technique was originally designed to help people recapture and relive their past lives, but, with minor changes, the same method can be used to astral travel.

Gerald Glaskin learned the technique from a small magazine called *Open Mind* and found that it completely transformed his life. He later wrote a number of books on the subject.[15]

The technique itself is simple, but three people are required. The person who is going to astral travel lies flat on the floor with his or her head supported by a small pillow. This person should be wearing loose-fitting clothes and no shoes. I'll call this person the "traveler."

The traveler closes his or her eyes and one of the other two people massages this person's ankles for a few minutes to help the traveler relax. Shortly after this massage begins, the third person massages the traveler's forehead in the area of the third eye. This area is in the lower center of the forehead, just above the eyebrows. The third person uses the edge of his curved hand and rubs vigorously.

While this is going on the traveler concentrates on relaxing. If necessary he or she can take several deep breaths to help the procedure along.

After a few minutes of this, one of the two assistants tells the traveler to become aware of his or her feet and to visualize them as clearly as possible. Then he or she is asked to visualize growing two inches taller through the bottoms of the feet. When the traveler feels or becomes aware that this has occurred he tells the assistant. The assistant then tells him to go back to his or her normal size.

This is repeated several times. The traveler is encouraged to talk about the feelings that occur as he or she is growing taller and returning to normal size again.

Once this has been done successfully, the traveler is then asked to imagine growing two inches taller out of the top of his or her head. This is also done several times.

After this, the traveler is asked to stretch twelve inches out of the bottom of his or her feet, and then return to normal size. This is repeated with the head.

Now the traveler is asked to extend twenty-four inches out of the bottom of his or her feet. This can be difficult for some people, and the assistant needs to be patient and encouraging. Once the feet have been extended, the traveler is asked to stretch twenty-four inches out the top of his or her head, without retracting the feet. Some people find it difficult to stretch out the top of their head without retracting their feet at the same time. Consequently, the assistant needs to be patient and may have to repeat this stage a number of times.

Once the traveler is extended two feet in each direction, he or she is then asked to expand the same amount in every direction. In other words, to expand like a giant balloon.

At this stage, the traveler will be virtually out of his or her body, but may not yet be aware of it.

The assistant now asks the traveler to visualize the front door of his or her home and to describe it out loud in detail. The assistant questions the traveler closely until satisfied that the door and its surroundings have been described adequately.

The assistant then asks the traveler to imagine standing on the roof of his or her home and to describe what he or she can see. The assistant asks for more and more information to encourage the traveler to "see" in detail with his or her eyes closed.

Once this has been done, the traveler is told to visualize flying 500 feet up into the air and then to go directly wherever he or she wants to go. (In the original "past life" version, the traveler descended to Earth in a different place and time at this point and started to relive a previous incarnation.)

The traveler reports on what he or she is seeing throughout the astral travel and the assistant helps by asking questions to gain as much detailed information as possible.

When the traveler feels ready to return, the assistant guides him or her back into the physical body. The traveler should lie there, eyes closed, for two or three minutes to become familiar with his or her surroundings.

This is certainly the safest way I know of astral traveling, because you are guided by the assistant throughout. The disadvantage of this method is that you need two like-minded assistants to help you.

Fortunately, this method can be done by yourself using self-hypnosis. You lose the advantage of being questioned and guided by the assistant, but at least you can travel whenever you wish, rather than waiting until your friends are available.

If you intend to use this method by yourself, you will need to learn self-hypnosis. This is a useful skill that you can learn in about a week if you use a book, and in about an hour if you are taught by a competent hypnotherapist. You will also need to prepare a tape that you can listen to. Start with a progressive relaxation and then move on to the stage of becoming taller through the feet and head. You can stop recording after reaching 500 feet into the air.

There is no danger of not returning from an experience of this sort. You will find that the astral travel will create its own logical finish and you will be back inside your body. You will find that each trip will seem to last five to ten minutes, but in actuality, will be some five times longer than that.

Hypnotism Method

I have used this method frequently with people who have found it difficult to leave their bodies in any other way. Hypnosis bypasses the conscious, critical factor of the logical, conscious mind and deals directly with the inner, subconscious mind. Consequently, people who have hidden fears of some sort may want to astral travel, and may experiment with the different methods, but somehow never quite succeed. Hypnosis can be very useful for these people.

There are two ways of using hypnotism. You can use self-hypnosis or find a qualified hypnotherapist who is interested in the psychic world. The second method is by far the better, as you will have a qualified professional to guide you out of the body and into your first out-of-body experience.

If that is not possible, you will have to learn self-hypnosis. There are many books available that will teach you the basics of this useful skill. If you have experimented with the previous methods you will be well on the way to learning self-hypnosis anyway, as progressive relaxation is often used as a method of entering hypnosis.

To astral travel directly from a progressive relaxation using hypnosis, you will have to practice relaxing as often as you can. Once you can do this quickly and easily, you need simply think about where you want to go and visualize yourself leaving your physical body. I prefer to imagine myself leaving through my forehead, just above the eyebrows.

Once you are aware that you are floating above your physical body, think of where you want to go, and go there.

In the 1970s, parapsychologists experimented with a combination of progressive relaxation, oscillating sounds, and a rotating spiral.[16] This spiral is available from novelty stores and is usually called a "hypno-disc."

To use it, you need to mount it on cardboard and attach it to a multi-speed electric drill. Place the drill several feet away from where you will be sitting, with the hypno-disc facing you. Start the drill on the lowest speed, sit down in a comfortable, recliner-type chair, gaze at the rotating disc, and go through a progressive relaxation with your eyes open. I find that baroque music, plus the sound of the drill, provides a suitably disorienting sound when accompanied by the hypno-disc. The interesting thing about this method is that many people find themselves plucked out of their bodies before they have even finished the progressive relaxation.

In the late nineteenth century, many people experimented with hypnotism as a means of leaving the body. One famous example was recorded in the *Proceedings* of the Society for Psychical Research.

Dr. F had been experimenting with what was called at the time "traveling clairvoyance." He arranged for Mr. Eglinton, one of his patients, to stay home on a certain night. He then hypnotized a woman named Jane and asked her to clairvoyantly call on the patient. Jane did not know Mr. Eglinton and had not even been to the district where he lived.

After she had been hypnotized, Dr. F asked her to go to the patient's apartment. She did so, accurately describing the entrance and the knocker on the front door. Inside the house, she accurately described the furnishings, but then apparently failed when she described the appearance of Mr. Eglinton. She said he was fat and had an artificial leg.

The next day, Dr. F learned that the patient had become tired of waiting and had gone out, after making a dummy of himself using clothes and pillows. He placed this in an armchair with a glass of brandy on one side and a pile of newspapers on the other. Consequently, Jane's description of a fat man with artificial limbs was correct.[17]

Although Dr. F considered this successful experiment to be "traveling clairvoyance," it was obviously an astral travel. If Jane had used clairvoyance she would have realized that the figure she saw was just a dummy and not a real person. Using astral travel, Jane would have seen the room and the person sitting in it, and simply not realized that the figure was not real.

You may find that one of these methods is perfect for you, and choose to use it every time. You may discover, as I did, that it is fun to use a variety of methods.

Do not give up after trying these one or two times. It takes time to learn any worthwhile skill. A friend of mine persevered for several months before finally succeeding using the Willpower method. The strange thing is that he had not attempted this method earlier because he thought that he had no willpower. Now he astral travels whenever he wishes.

Be calm, be patient, and keep on practicing. If you do, you will ultimately succeed.

Chapter Ten

Astral Traveling in Your Sleep

YOU ALREADY KNOW THAT WE REGULARLY ASTRAL travel in our sleep. One of the main problems of leaving the body in this way is that we seldom remember the experiences afterwards. This is a quandary, particularly as many of the experts from the past recommend learning how to astral travel this way.

The trick is to fall asleep physically, but to somehow also keep the conscious mind awake. Some people are able to do this without even thinking about it.

I remember, as a child, having long conversations with my younger sister when she was asleep. Even though she was sound asleep, she would hear and respond to questions put to her. The fascinating part of the exercise was that she always told the truth while talking in her sleep, and my brother, sister, and I learned a great deal about her real feelings on a variety of different subjects.

As an adult, I have occasionally implanted positive suggestions to people while they were asleep. Sometimes this involved holding conversations with them, even though they were sound asleep. In most cases, I had to talk gently and bring them up to an almost awake stage before starting to give them the positive suggestions that they needed. However, a few of them were able to understand and answer in their sleep, in exactly the same way as my sister did.

Many years ago, I prepared a tape to help people fall asleep and then go on an astral travel. You can very easily create one for yourself. You need to start with a progressive relaxation that sends the person to sleep, and immediately follow this with suggestions that the person will leave his or her body and go on an astral travel.

When I started experimenting with this, I would sit on a chair beside the bed and guide the person into sleep. Once he or she was asleep, I would then continue with the out-of-body suggestions. I did it this way because some people fall asleep quickly and easily, but other people take time. However, I found that, by using a progressive relaxation technique, almost everyone falls asleep within ten minutes, and it does not matter if the voice continues giving suggestions about falling asleep once the person has nodded off. This meant that I could record the suggestions on cassette and experiment with a much wider range of people.

If you make a tape for yourself, choose some gentle background music to play quietly while you record the following script. It is best if the music does not contain any recognizable melodies, as these can provoke memories and start the mind thinking about them rather than concentrating on relaxing. There is a huge range of New Age music available nowadays and it is great fun listening to a selection and finally choosing something that you like.

You do not need to follow my suggested script slavishly. You may already have your own favorite method of relaxing. If so, use that, as you are already familiar with it and know that it produces the desired result. You may prefer one of the other progressive relaxation scripts in this book. If so, use it. You may want to sit down and create your own script. That is fine, too. Just use whatever works for you.

Once you have made your cassette, go to bed in your usual manner. Once you turn out the light and prepare for sleep, turn your cassette machine on and follow along with the suggestions. You do not need to try hard. In fact, if you try too hard, it will make it more difficult to fall asleep. Your mind will drift away from time to time. When you become aware of this, simply focus on the words again. It does not matter if you hear very few of the words. Your subconscious, inner mind will be receiving them anyway, and that is all that matters.

When you wake up after falling asleep this way, record your impressions as quickly as possible. Do this whether you feel that you have astral traveled during the night or not. Sometimes, as soon as you start writing, you will realize that you have actually astral traveled in your sleep after all.

This is a highly effective way of astral traveling. I find that when I do it, I wake up while out of my body and instantly go back to sleep as soon as I return. Some people experience it more as a dream and say that they do not wake up, even though they have complete recall of the travel the next morning.

Occasionally, I am asked if this is really astral travel when it occurs while the person is asleep. Yes, it is a valid astral travel. When you astral travel you are extremely aware of everything that is going on. The colors are more intense and vivid, and you feel more alive than you do during the day. These things do not happen in a dream.

Even though the astral travels you experience using this script occur in your sleep, they are induced travels, and not the usual type of astral travel we all regularly have in our sleep. Consequently, you are more likely to remember them in the morning.

Astral Travel in Your Sleep Script

It's so good to be in bed, ready for a good night's sleep. You're going to fall asleep so easily, so quickly tonight and you're going to astral travel in your sleep. You know exactly where you want to astral travel.

Pause for fifteen seconds here to allow the person to think about the place to which he or she intends to travel.

Take a nice deep breath in now and, as you exhale, allow a wave of relaxation to drift right through you, from the top of your head to the tips of your toes.

It's so good to relax in bed. You're ready for sleep and each breath you take makes you more and more relaxed. And the more relaxed you become, the sleepier you get. And the sleepier you become, the more relaxed you find yourself.

Take another deep breath in and, as you exhale, picture yourself in your mind's eye, already asleep. You can see your chest moving rhythmically up and down as you take slow, deep breaths. You can see how peaceful and totally relaxed you are, as you allow that beneficial sleep to restore every cell of your body. It's so good to sleep deeply and soundly like that.

Just drifting and floating, so peacefully, with nothing to bother or disturb you. And each breath you take sends you deeper and deeper into this wonderful world of total, complete, absolute relaxation.

Just as if you're lying back on a fluffy cloud, floating along and relaxing as you watch the earth below. It's a nice feeling, a comfortable feeling and you're becoming more relaxed with each easy breath you take.

Picture yourself now in a comfortable rocking chair. You're sitting on a long, shady verandah and you're looking out on the most indescribably beautiful scene you have ever set eyes on. It's a hot day, but in the shade of the veranda it's so, so pleasant and you look out on the scene in a sleepy, half-awake manner.

As the chair rocks back and forth, seemingly under its own volition, your eyes seem so heavy and you can feel the relaxation spreading through every part of your body as you gently rock yourself to sleep.

Yes. You're ready for sleep now and although you're still rocking gently in that comfortable rocking chair, your eyes are closed and you're drifting and floating without a care in the world.

And as you're drifting and floating in this comfortable chair, it seems as if the chair is floating, too. It seems just an inch or two off the ground. And then you realize that it is floating, and this makes you even more relaxed.

The chair slowly glides across the veranda and, when it reaches the steps leading down to a beautiful, crisp, green, manicured lawn, it gives a gentle shake, and then you're moving outward and upwards at the same time.

It's so peaceful and calm, sitting in this rocking chair as it floats gently upwards and you can see the gorgeous landscape below you.

And the chair is moving faster now. It's funny, but as the chair gains speed, you become more and more relaxed. More and more relaxed. So comfortable. So contented. And so, so relaxed.

You can feel the cool breeze as it caresses your toes and relaxes them still more. The breeze relaxes your feet now. It's a soft, gentle, warm breeze and it soothes and relaxes you as it gently massages both of your feet.

The breeze is now relaxing your calves and knees, and you realize again how wonderful, soothing, peaceful, and relaxing it is to be floating effortlessly through space on this beautiful, comfortable rocking chair.

The sky is an incredible blue today and the small puffs of fluffy, white clouds seem to be dancing and playing as you head towards them.

Your thighs are relaxing now, and you realize that your legs are so relaxed, so completely relaxed, that you are hardly aware of them anymore. Moving your legs seems to be the very last thing you'd want to do now.

Looking down now from this wonderful, comfortable armchair, you can see the coastline far below you. You can see the beaches and the waves rolling in and out. And as those waves roll in and out, you can feel yourself relaxing along with them, relaxing a thousand times more than before.

That soft, gentle breeze is now drifting into your stomach and up, up into your chest. Your stomach and chest are so relaxed now, just as relaxed as your legs.

Feel your shoulder muscles relax as the breeze reaches up to kiss them. That relaxation drifts down your arms now. Your arms feel so heavy and loose and lazy. The breeze relaxes your hands and every finger, squeezing out every last trace of tension and stress and worry.

It's so peaceful and calm to be in this relaxing rocking chair as you float gently out to sea.

The breeze is touching your neck and face now, sending pleasant relaxation into every part of your body. Feel the muscles around your jaw and mouth relax. Feel the muscles around your eyes as they relax, too. And let that pleasant relaxation drift up into your scalp, so that you are now totally relaxed from the top of your head down to the tips of your toes.

You are so relaxed now, and sleep is coming. It's not far away now. And you can feel the rocking chair coming down a bit now as you dream and float through space and time, leaving all your cares, all your worries far behind.

As you look down now, you can see a beautiful tropical island below you. It is surrounded with gorgeous, golden sand. Below you is a beautiful lagoon. You can see the waves as they pound on the coral reef. It's a pleasant sound that makes you even more relaxed.

The rocking chair settles down on the beautiful, warm sand. It's so quiet and peaceful. You lazily reach over and pick up a handful of that golden sand. You trickle it between your fingers. It's so restful here. You have all the time in the world to just relax.

You can hear the breeze as it rustles through the palm trees. In the distance, the sound of the waves crashing rhythmically onto the reef makes you even more relaxed. The gentle, warm sun caresses your skin.

It's so beautiful, so peaceful, so restful. You could fall asleep here and have the best sleep of your life. And in your dream you'd eat the beautiful tropical fruits and drink their juices. You'd swim in the inviting lagoon and lie on the warm sand. And you'd wake up in the morning completely invigorated.

You're totally relaxed now. All your muscles are loose and limp and asleep. Your body is relaxed, completely relaxed from the top of your head to the tips of your toes.

And you're letting yourself go. Drifting into sleep now. Restful sleep. Pleasant, enjoyable sleep. The rocking chair is now rocking gently, sending you into sleep. And as you drift into a pleasant, relaxing sleep, it starts to float up into the air again. Higher and higher. As it goes, it rocks almost imperceptibly, and each rocking motion sends you deeper, and deeper, and deeper, and deeper into sleep.

It's high over the ocean again now, but you're scarcely aware of it as it feels so good to just sleep, sleep, sleep. You're flying gently over the land now, coming down very slowly, as if it were in a dream, and now you're hovering over that beautiful scene and coming in to land on the cool, shady veranda that you left—how long ago was it?

And as you rock gently to and fro on the veranda of the beautiful house, overlooking that gorgeous scene, it seems almost like a dream. To think that you floated through the air on your rocking chair and visited strange and exotic places.

It's wonderful to think that you can recapture this complete and utter restfulness and total tranquility any time you want. This feeling of comfort and total security. This feeling of well-being. This feeling of love. Love both given and received. Pure, unconditional love that makes you feel better than you've felt in a long, long time.

It's strange to think that you traveled over the oceans in a rocking chair, but you know you have the ability to travel anywhere you wish, at any time at all.

See yourself sleeping peacefully in that rocking chair, and as you watch, see your astral double escaping and floating up higher and higher, looking down on your physical body fast asleep in the comfortable, relaxing rocking chair.

See yourself floating higher and higher, looking down on yourself in the rocking chair, as it gets smaller and smaller. And now you are floating free, able to fly wherever you wish.

Enjoy the sensation of exhilaration this feeling of freedom gives. From here you can look down on the fields, the orchards, the houses, the villages. Even towns as you float higher and higher.

You could drift and float like this all night, because the feeling is one of perfect peace and contentment. But you know that you can go anywhere you wish, anywhere at all. And you can do it instantly. All you need do is think where you want to go and you'll be there.

Think now of where you want to go.

Pause for fifteen seconds.

That's right, that's it. You're now there!

Look around. Familiarize yourself with the scene. See who's there and what they're doing. See everything in glorious, crisp, bright colors. Feel the environment and scene in every pore of your being. Smell the smells, feel the temperature, hear the sounds, and understand it all.

Realize that you will remember absolutely everything that happens during this astral travel. You are free of the physical and can do anything and go wherever you wish. You are safe, secure, and protected. You are in total control. Nothing can harm you in any way. You can return anytime you wish, or you might stay here longer and see and learn more. Or you might choose to go somewhere else, just by thinking about it. It's up to you.

And when you're ready, you can instantly return to your physical body again just by thinking of it. And when you're back, you'll go deeper and deeper into pleasant, enjoyable, beneficial sleep. And you'll wake up at your predetermined time in the morning feeling like a million dollars. You'll be refreshed, revitalized, and ready for a dynamic, productive day. And you'll also wake up with a clear recall of where you've been and what you've done in your sleep.

Stay as long as you wish, and then simply think about returning and you'll be back. And you can do this again and again and again, anytime you wish.

Do not expect miracles the first time you do this. Hopefully, you will wake up with a full recall of everything that happened. However, you may also wake up and not remember anything.

If this happens, sit down with pen and paper, close your eyes and see what comes into your mind. Write down anything that comes into your consciousness. Usually, this will prompt your recall and you will be able to record your astral travel. Do not worry if nothing comes back. Simply try again the following night and the night after, until you do remember.

Chapter Eleven

Traveling in Pairs

SEVERAL YEARS AGO A YOUNG COUPLE CAME TO ME because they wanted to be regressed back to a past life. They were deeply in love and were convinced that they must have been together in several previous lifetimes. It was an interesting situation and I was just as curious as they were to see how they had been related to each other in past lives.

Unfortunately, though they both gave detailed accounts of several previous lifetimes, neither figured in any of the other's memories of previous lives. This was disappointing and they made an appointment for a future life progression. This worried them, also, because they became concerned that they might not be together in their next life. Consequently, a few days later, they phoned and changed the appointment to an astral travel.

This was the first time I had been asked to help a couple take an astral trip together. In my classes I had helped groups of people to astral travel, but they went wherever they wished, and always to different places. It was an intriguing idea to guide a couple through the same astral travel experience, and I was probably as excited about the idea as they were.

When they arrived for their appointment, they said that they wanted to astral travel to Burma. Fortunately, I had a photographic guide book that included Burma as well as several other countries. Using this, we determined the places the couple wanted to visit, and set out on the trip.

I was not concerned about their ability to leave their physical bodies. They had been excellent hypnotic subjects, and I have found that these people usually find it easy to astral travel. However, I was a little bit concerned about guiding them through the entire experience, as they would be able to experience everything, but I would be guessing as to where they were and what they would be doing at any given moment. I also thought that one might want to explore a certain place in greater depth than the other, which might cause them to suddenly return to their physical bodies or become frustrated. I also felt that my voice might be a distraction, forcing them to move on at places that interested them, and holding them back at places of little interest.

In fact, I had nothing to worry about. They left their bodies easily and I managed to guide them through the experience at the right pace. They were so thrilled that they came back several times to take other trips

Since then, I have helped many couples make a joint astral travel. The first two talked about it to their friends and that brought other people to me. I have had a few instances in which one partner left the body but the other one didn't, but apart from that have had no problems. For most people it was their first astral travel, and many have commented on how "safe" the experience felt. Most of them have since astral traveled on their own because they enjoyed the experience so much.

You can either record a script on cassette, or have a third person guide the other two through the experience. It is better if three people are involved. The advantage of this is that he or she can watch the other two and either speed up or slow down the initial progressive relaxation stage. Also, hypnotherapists have discovered that people relax much more easily and deeply when listening to a "real" person than when listening to a cassette. No one knows the reason for this, but everyone who has attended a hypnosis session and then listened to tapes knows that this is the case.

Naturally, the third person needs to be someone whom you trust implicitly. He or she will also need to have a pleasant speaking voice and be able to read the script with expression. If the person sounds as if he or she is reading from a script, the success rate is much lower. This is the case even when you know that this is what the person is doing. I am sure you have had the experience of someone trying to sell you something over the phone using a badly written script that was obviously

being read. I am sure you didn't buy, and in fact, probably felt rather annoyed at being bothered by the call. If
you cannot find someone you trust who has a pleasant,
well-modulated speaking voice, you will have to make
yourself a script and record it on cassette.

You will have to agree on where you want to go and
what you want to do, so that the third person will know
where to direct you to go.

Here is a sample script for a trip into outer space. It is
best if the script is not read word for word. When I
guide someone on an astral travel in this way, I do not
use a script as such, but use notes to keep me on track.
That way I can spend as much time as is necessary on
the initial relaxation before my clients leave their bodies.

I have also included a different form of relaxation for
you to try. You may prefer it to the progressive relaxation in Chapter Four. I find it good to have a choice, as
it means I can alternate whenever I wish.

You can also use any of the methods described earlier
to leave the body. Again, I have included another version here that utilizes moving the conscious mind. I find
that this version works very well for couples and groups.

Naturally, the two people who are about to astral travel need to sit back or recline in a comfortable chair in a
warm room. Any clothing should be as loose as possible.
The room needs to be darkened, but not necessarily
dark, especially if the third person is going to be reading
a script. This third person needs to be sitting upright
and facing the two participants. By watching them, he or
she will have some idea as to how relaxed they are and
whether or not the experiment is succeeding.

Relaxation Procedure

Sit back comfortably, close your eyes, and take a deep breath in. Hold it for a few seconds and let it out slowly. Feel yourself relax all over as you exhale. Take another deep breath, hold it for a few moments, and again let it out slowly. Feel the relaxation from the top of your head to the tips of your toes.

Become aware of your toes. Wiggle them a little. Good, and now clench them tightly. Feel the tension in your toes as you clench them. Now relax your toes and feel the wonderful relaxation drift back into your toes.

Clench your feet now, as much as you can. Hold it for a moment or two, and then relax your feet.

Think of your calf muscles. Clench them tightly, tighter and tighter. Hold them like that for a few seconds and then—relax! Feel the relaxation in every part of your body that is below your knees.

Bring your attention up over your knees and into your thighs. Clench your thighs and your buttocks. Clench them as tightly as you can. So tight. Feel the tension in your thighs and buttocks. Hold them like that, hold them, hold them, and now—relax! Feel how relaxed your thighs and buttocks are.

Squeeze your abdominal muscles. Tighter, tighter now. Hold them a few seconds and then let go. Allow your abdomen to relax as much as it can.

Now clench your fingers and arms. Imagine they are like iron bars, so firm and rigid and tight. Squeeze your hands even more tightly. Good. Hold it, hold it—and let go! Let your arms and hands relax.

Tighten your shoulder muscles now. So tight that it feels as if you've had a really tough day at work. That's good, that's very good! Let go now. Let your shoulders go.

See how tight you can make your neck muscles go. Tighter, tighter, that's good. Hold them for a few seconds. Release the tension and relax.

Clench your jaw now. Tighter than that. So tight that you think it might clamp shut forever. Good. Now relax and let it go.

Now it's the turn of your eyes. The muscles around your eyes are the finest muscles in your whole body. Tighten them now. Squeeze your eyes, tightly, tightly shut. Hold them like that for a while, and, now, let go and relax.

Feel that relaxation right through your body, and you're becoming more relaxed with every easy breath you take. Now we're going to tense

again, on the count of three. When I reach
three I want you to tense every part of your
body, so that you're clenched tightly all over.
Ready now, one, two, three! Tighten up!
Clench feet, legs, buttocks, arms, shoulders,
neck, jaw, and eyes. Hold that tension. Hold it
until I count to three. When I reach three,
relax everything all at the same time. Ready
now—one, two, three! Relax. Every part of
your body is relaxing, relaxing, relaxing.

Cast an eye over your entire body. If any part
seems at all tense, tighten it for a moment and
then let it go. You want every part of your body
to be as loose and relaxed as possible.

That's good. You're now loose, limp, and
relaxed in every part of your body. I'm going to
test you now. In a moment I'm going to lift up
one of your arms. Just think about relaxing,
relaxing, relaxing. No thought in your mind
other than this wonderful, joyful feeling of
total relaxation.

The guide waits about thirty seconds and then lifts up
an arm of one of the subjects. It is best to pick it up at
the wrist and raise it just a few inches. When the guide
lets go the arm should flop loosely down, as if it were
totally lifeless. This is repeated with the other person. If
both arms are totally relaxed, the guide can move on to
the next part of the experiment. If not, the participants

are not relaxed enough, and the guide will have to go through the previous exercise again. Once both participants are totally relaxed, the procedure can continue.

Leaving the Body

It's now time to leave the physical body behind, and to begin with, I'd like you to become aware of your conscious mind. Just be aware of the inner computer that leads its own life inside your body. Most of the time it's your best friend, guiding and advising you every moment of your life.

Become aware of your conscious mind and move it down through your body. Move your conscious mind down into the area of your stomach. Visualize it there, feel it there, and sense it there. Notice how it just keeps on working wherever it happens to be.

Move it now into your right hand. Choose a finger and visualize your conscious mind inside that finger. See it, feel it, until it becomes real. Your conscious mind can be anywhere you want it to be.

Let it go back to its normal home now. That's good. Now, quickly, move it back to that finger again.

Pause.

Home.

Pause.

Back to the finger.

Pause.

Home.

Pause.

Back to the finger. That's good!
Move it now to your right knee. See how
quickly you can move it there. Now move it to
your other knee. Good. Now move it back
again to your right knee.

Pause.

Left knee now.

Pause.

Right knee.

Pause.

Left knee.

Pause.

Your finger.

Pause.

Abdomen.

Pause.

And home.

Very good. You're doing well. We're going to take it a step further now and move your conscious mind out of your body. In your mind's eye picture a child's cuddly toy. It might be a cuddly toy you owned as a child. It might be one you've seen somewhere. It might be something you simply make up. Picture it as clearly as you can. See the colors. You might even be able to smell it.

Now mentally place that cuddly toy on the floor beside you. Good. Become aware of your conscious mind again and place it inside the cuddly toy. Again, imagine it, visualize it, and feel it happening. Notice that your conscious mind keeps on working, but now it's doing it from inside your cuddly toy.

Move it back to its normal place again now. Good. And now back to the cuddly toy. Back home. And to the cuddly toy. Notice that it's becoming easier and easier to do. Move it back home again now.

That's very good. Move it now into my right shoe. Visualize it inside my right shoe. That's right. That's right. It's now inside my right shoe. Now send it back home. Yes, and now back to my shoe. And back home again.

You've seen how your conscious mind can keep on functioning and working wherever it happens to be. It can be anywhere in the universe and still look after you. We're going to prove that to you in just a moment.

Before we do that, we'll just do one more thing with your conscious mind. Visualize a room at home or work. See it as clearly as you can. Choose an object in that room and send your conscious mind there. That's quick! Very good. Send it home again now. Back to that object, and then back home.

We're now ready to move on. Become aware of the area in the center of your forehead just above your eyes. Visualize that area slowly revolving in a circle. Round and round. Round and round. Gradually moving faster and faster as it goes around and around.

You're opening up your third eye now. Visualize a fine stream of energy coming out of your third eye. It's fine, like a fine mist. As it comes out it takes on your shape. You are building up your astral double. See it coming on out, coming on out, coming on out until it becomes life-size. It's almost there now. A little bit more—and, yes, it's there. Your astral double is standing beside you, waiting for your

instructions. Picture your astral double, the same size and shape as you, waiting patiently.

Become aware of your consciousness yet again. Good. Now place your consciousness into your astral double. Notice how it still works the way it always does, even though it is now inside your astral double.

Now we're ready to begin.

Visit to Outer Space

At this point you can send the couple anywhere they wish to go. The following trip into space is purely for example purposes only. I have found that sending a couple into space works very well for their first astral travel together. Once they have done that successfully, it is much easier for them to astral travel to other places.

Your astral double is ready to go wherever you wish. It contains your conscious mind and will always be connected to you by a silver cord. Your astral double can be recalled to your physical body any time you wish. And it will return instantly. Before you can say the word "return" it will be back.

On the count of three I want you both to take a nice deep breath. Hold it until I tell you to exhale. As you let your breath out you will find yourself instantly transported into space.

Ready, one, two, three. Breathe in. Hold it, hold it, and exhale slowly.

Feel yourself now, floating effortlessly through space. You are warm, comfortable, relaxed, and a little bit excited. You can see your partner floating beside you. There is the Moon on your right. Move a bit closer to get a good look at it as you sail past. See all the planets and stars before you as you move deeper and deeper into outer space. Nothing need disturb or bother you. You are so calm and relaxed. It's peaceful, tranquil, and quiet.

Now we're getting close to Mars. You want to stop here for a while and see what it's like. Take note of everything you see and hear. What's your partner looking at now? Sit down together and rest for a little while. You really get a different perspective on everything when you sit down on another planet and look around. Doesn't Earth look small and far away?

It's time to move on again. You can see Jupiter far in the distance. It's the largest planet in this particular solar system. Let's head there and see what it's like. That was quick! Isn't it wonderful to be able to travel through space instantaneously? Pause and have a rest again. You might want to walk around hand-in-hand and explore. It's perfectly safe, and you enjoy walking around and exploring Jupiter.

We have time to look at only one more planet today. It would be fun to visit Saturn and see what the rings are made of. Again, see everything as clearly as you can. Look at the rings closely. They're made of small frozen particles. What do they feel like? And now fly through and have a look at the planet itself. Do you prefer it to Mars and Jupiter? It certainly has a different atmosphere and feeling about it.

This is so much fun we could explore the different galaxies forever, but it is getting late and soon it will be time to return. Take a quick trip out to see some stars. See yourselves flying hand-in-hand through time and space. Flying, floating effortlessly.

And now see yourself returning, returning, returning. Back through time and space and now you are sitting in this room again. Your astral double is beside you. Visualize your consciousness returning home. That's good. And now see your astral double returning through your third eye until it has completely disappeared.

You are relaxed, totally relaxed, and in a moment I'll count from one to five. When I reach

five, you'll open your eyes feeling wonderful in every way and remembering absolutely everything that happened during your trip away.

One, gaining energy and feeling happy. Two, mind so clear and memory perfect. Three, energy returning to every part of your body. Four, feeling better than you've felt in ages. And five, eyes opening and feeling great.

It is a good idea to ask both people to write down their experiences before they start talking about them. That way, they will have conclusive evidence that they traveled together and did the same things. Usually, though, the two people cannot wait to start talking about their experiences. This is quite understandable, of course. After all, it is not every day that you get the opportunity to travel around the universe with your partner!

One wonderful side benefit of astral traveling with a partner is that it seems to bring the two people even closer together. Almost every couple I have worked with has experienced this.

Naturally, this method is not restricted to couples. You can use it to guide one person through an astral travel. This is a particularly good method to use if the person has some subconscious fears about astral travel.

Although I have not done it myself, this method could also be used for small groups of, say, three or four people. The next chapter contains a method of sending larger groups of people on an astral trip.

Chapter Twelve

Group Astral Travel

ONCE YOU HAVE MASTERED THE ART OF ASTRAL traveling and discovered how stimulating and rewarding it can be, you may want to help other people learn how to leave their physical bodies as well. If you decide to do this, start with a group of people who are interested in psychic matters. It does not matter if they know nothing at all about astral projection, but they must have a genuine interest in the paranormal. Later on, when you have gained confidence and experience, you can offer astral travels to any group that expresses interest.

Let's assume that you are guiding a group of seven or eight people through their first astral travel. You have asked them to bring cushions and blankets, and to wear comfortable, loose-fitting clothes.

Start by asking them what they expect from the experience. You may be surprised at some of the answers you receive. On one occasion an elderly lady told me that she wanted to astral travel to find the soul of her dead cat! Most people will simply be curious to see if they can astral travel, and if so, what the experience will be like.

Once they have told you this, it is your turn. Tell them what you know about astral travel and how you became interested in the subject. Tell them about your first few experiences in the astral plane. Emphasize how safe the experience is and how enjoyable it will be.

Ask for any questions. After answering these, ask everyone to stand up and stretch before making themselves as comfortable as they can on the floor or chairs. It does not matter what position they choose. They can lie on the floor or sit back in a chair, but their arms and legs are not to be crossed.

Dim the light and put on some gentle meditation music. Do not do as I did on one occasion and play sounds of nature. The sound of trickling water made everyone want to use the bathroom! Once everyone is comfortable, have them go through a simple relaxation exercise.

Take a nice, deep breath in and close your eyes as you slowly let it out. Take another deep breath, and exhale slowly. That's good. Nice, deep breaths. Relax as much as you can. You'll find that every breath you take makes you more and more relaxed. It's so pleasant to

simply relax and let the world go by. All you need do is relax.

Feel the relaxation drifting over your face. Relax the muscles around your eyes. Relax them as much as you can. Relax your jaw muscles and feel your whole face totally relaxed, totally relaxed and at peace.

Allow this pleasant relaxation to drift into your neck now. Allow your neck to completely relax. Let this wonderful feeling of relaxation drift into your shoulders. We all gather stress and tension here, so let your shoulders completely relax. That's good. Let the relaxation drift down both arms. Feel the relaxation as it goes down, down, down to the tips of your fingers. Feel your hands and fingers as they totally relax.

Let your chest relax, and then let that relaxation move down to your abdomen, relaxing, relaxing, relaxing as it goes.

Let your legs relax now. Feel the pleasant relaxation in your thighs, then let it go over your knees and into your calves and ankles. Now let your feet relax.

Take a nice deep breath in again and, as you exhale, let a wave of relaxation go right through your entire body.

Mentally, check your body and make sure that every part is totally, completely relaxed. If any part is still tense, focus on it and allow it to relax.

You are now completely relaxed and you are ready for the exciting experiences ahead. In your mind's eye picture yourself in your teenage years. Select a scene from your past and focus in on it. Become aware of what was going on, who was there, and how you felt about the situation. It makes no difference if the scene was a happy one or a sad one. Just as long as you can recapture it in your mind. You might see it, or perhaps feel it, or just capture the emotions from it. It does not matter.

Let that scene go now and picture yourself at work or study. If you are a student, you might picture a lecture room or the library. If you are in the work force, picture yourself doing whatever it is you do to make your living. Again, visualize it as clearly as you can. That's excellent. Now let it go. I'm sorry to take you to work, even for a few brief seconds.

Finally, visualize yourself as clearly as you can, in a space capsule which is about to land on the Moon. See what you're doing, what's happening outside as you get closer and closer to the Moon's surface. Feel and sense everything that's going on.

Very good. Now let go of that, too, and return to the comfort and security of this room. In a moment I'm going to count from one to five. When I reach five, you'll open your eyes feeling refreshed, revitalized, and full of energy.

One, coming up a little bit now. Two, gaining energy and feeling great. Three, becoming aware of the situation inside the room. Four, your whole body rested and restored, and five—eyes opening!

Wait until everyone has his or her eyes open and is looking alert. Ask each one how they felt about the relaxation procedure. Most will have enjoyed it. One or two might have found it slightly strange. Tell them that when doing a deliberate relaxation exercise like the one they have just done, every single cell in their body relaxes.

The main purpose of this initial procedure is to get everybody to relax. This also has the benefit of making them feel more comfortable. You will probably notice people talking more freely at this stage than they were at the beginning. This is because they are now relaxed and have shared a ritual of sorts with everyone else in the room.

They have also had an opportunity to visualize the pictures you put into their minds. Some will have found the Moon landing to be the easiest to visualize, but others will have pictured the other two scenes more easily. This tells you how imaginative your group is.

Ask everyone to stand up and stretch again before moving on to the next stage. They will all find it easier to relax this time, so that part of the exercise can be briefer than before.

Take a nice, deep breath in, and close your eyes as you exhale. Let a wave of relaxation drift right through your body, from the top of your head to the tips of your toes. That's good. Relaxing more and more with each easy breath.

Picture yourself now at the top of a beautiful staircase. It is the most beautiful staircase you have ever seen, and it sweeps down in a curve to a magnificent room full of beautiful antiques and comfortable-looking furniture.

There are ten steps on this staircase. Place your hand on the handrail, and slowly go down the steps, one at a time. You'll double your relaxation with every count, so that by the time we reach the room below you'll be totally, absolutely r-e-l-a-x-e-d. Ten. You are relaxing more and more with every breath you take. Nine. Drifting and floating in a wonderfully peaceful state. Eight. Lower and lower. So calm and so relaxed. Seven. Drifting down still further. Six. Doubling your relaxation with every count. Five. You are halfway down now. Four. Drifting down still further. Three. Lower and lower. So, so relaxed. Two, and one.

As you walk down the last step onto the beautiful, deep-pile carpet of this magnificent room you feel a hundred times more relaxed than ever before. You move over to a comfort-able armchair and lie back in it, totally relaxed and happy.

And in this nice, calm, peaceful, relaxed state you are aware that we all experience many thousands of thoughts every day. Between fifty and sixty thousand of them, in fact. These thoughts come and go in our minds and we usually let them come and go as they wish. We seldom try to control them.

Today, though, we are going to do it. We are going to take total control over our thoughts by using a famous mantra. It is just a single word: OM. I'll have you say it, or rather, breathe it every time you exhale for the next few minutes. First, we'll coordinate everyone's breathing, so, on the count of three I want you to breathe in together. One, two, and three. Good, and say "Om" as you exhale. That's good. Breathe in again, and say the mantra as you exhale. Good. Now keep doing that for a few minutes. I'll get out of your way and let you concentrate on this mantra. I'll come back when it is time to stop.

In fact, you do not leave. You just sit quietly watching the students as they breathe in and out. Do not keep them doing it for too long. Between three and five min-utes is about the right length of time.

172 • Astral Travel for Beginners

**Okay, we'll stop saying the mantra now, and
on the count of five, you'll open your eyes
invigorated and ready for anything.**

**One, and two, and three, and four, and five.
Wide awake and feeling great.**

Wait until everyone has completely returned and
then ask them one at a time to tell the group about their
experiences during the exercise. You will be surprised at
the range of replies you receive. Some people will have
experienced fear, while others felt exulted. One or two
might not have experienced anything. Sometimes one or
two of them seem to experience a partial astral travel
Most will have seen colors or patterns moving in front
of their eyes. Some will have experienced a sinking feeling, which is often the first sign of an astral travel about
to start.

After this, have a break of at least ten minutes. This
gives people time to stretch their legs, visit the bathroom, and talk to the others about what has happened
so far.

Allow them to drink fruit juice or water, but not tea,
coffee, or alcohol. Likewise, cigarettes, marijuana, and
any other intoxicating substances have to be avoided. It
is better if people do not eat at this time, but a piece of
fruit is fine, if the person absolutely has to eat something. Chocolate, in particular, must be avoided.

When everyone is ready to start again, tell them
something about the astral body and how it is always
connected to the physical body. Stress that it can easily
be summoned back to the physical body at any time.

This time, the relaxation stage is even easier and faster. Ask everyone to lie or sit down with their eyes closed. Then have them extend their arms in front of themselves. This means up in the air for the people lying on their backs.

I'm going to count from five down to one. When I reach "one," let your arms and hands drop to your sides and allow a wave of relaxation to drift right through you, from the top of your head to the tips of your toes. Five. Four. Three. Two. One.

Watch as everyone lets their arms fall to their sides. Some will simply drop down, as if their arms were those of a rag doll. Others, though, will gradually lower their arms to their sides. These ones are not yet relaxed enough. Go to these people, one at a time, and raise both their hands up in the air. Hold their hands in yours and gently shake them, saying, "Relax, relax, relax." You will feel their arms becoming noticeably more relaxed. When you feel the time is right, let go, and their arms should drop down limply. The people who relaxed immediately will simply think that your words are directed to the group, rather than to individuals. When you are certain that everyone is relaxed you can continue.

We all have what is known as an astral double. This is a replica of our physical body and it can travel anywhere in the universe in a fraction of a second. We are going to separate our astral bodies from our physical bodies in just a moment.

Become aware of your forehead, in the area just above your eyes. This area is known as the "third eye." As you focus on this area, and concentrate on it, imagine it revolving, slowly at first, but then revolving faster and faster as it gains momentum. Notice that you can make it revolve at any speed you wish.

I now want you to imagine a mist or film of light coming out of your third eye. As it gathers it seems like a light, fluffy cloud. As more mist appears it seems to take on your shape, until it forms a life-sized replica of you made of this light, almost transparent film. Notice that it is attached to you through your third eye.

Notice also that you can retract it whenever you wish. Visualize it disappearing as it returns to your physical body through the third eye.

And now it is gone. Visualize it coming back now, much more quickly this time. Just practice moving it in and out a few times.

Keep silent for a couple of minutes while they practice.

Good. And return it to your physical body as we are going to come back now. Your astral double has completely returned and you will return to full conscious awareness as I count from one up to five.

One, and two, and three, and four and five.

Again ask everyone to describe what they felt or saw during that experience. The answers will be interesting. Some may have embarked on an astral travel while you paused to let them experiment. By this stage, all of them should be able to visualize their astral bodies. If one or two have not succeeded in this, give the others a ten or fifteen minute break and quickly repeat this section for the ones who need it. You want everyone to have visualized his or her astral double before you move on to the final stage, which is the astral travel itself.

The final relaxation exercise is the easiest of all. Simply ask them to hold their arms out, as before, close their eyes and, when they are ready, simply let them drop and instantly relax all over. Watch them as they do this, in case you need to help anyone to relax completely.

Once they have done this, wait a few seconds and then continue.

Good. You are now totally relaxed and each breath sends you even deeper and deeper into pleasant relaxation.

Activate your third eye now. Watch it revolve and then allow your astral double to come out. Watch it take shape as it appears. If you want to, you can send it back and bring it out again, but there is no need for that, as you already know that you can do it.

Become aware of your conscious mind. You might need to quiet it by silently saying a mantra to yourself. When you are ready, simply

move your conscious mind into your astral double. This is easier than it sounds. Simply visualize it inside your astral double.

Pause.

And now it is there.

Picture your astral body in a corner of the room. Any corner. Simply choose one and your astral double will immediately be there. Notice how you are still in touch with your conscious-ness, even though it is now many feet away from you.

Bring your astral double back so it is now beside you. In a moment I am going to have you think of somewhere you want to visit and your astral body will immediately be there. However, your physical body will be perfectly safe, and your astral body can return immedi-ately in the unlikely event of an emergency.

When you return, lie quietly for a minute or two before opening your eyes, and then keep as quiet as possible, because some of the others may still be out of their bodies.

All right now. Think of where you want to go, and now—go there!

Your task is virtually over now. Keep an eye on every-one and make sure that the first ones to return keep quiet, so as not to disturb the others who are still out of their bodies.

Frequently, you will find that one or two people stay away much longer than the others. If this carries on more than five minutes after everyone else has returned, you will need to gently guide them back into their bodies.

You have had a wonderful time. But it is time to return to your conscious mind. However, you know that you will be able to leave your body whenever you wish from now on. Right now, though, you are returning, returning, returning to your physical body. And you are now there. You are now back in your physical body.

Pause for thirty seconds.

On the count of five, you'll open your eyes and feel wonderful about the whole experience. One, memory perfect, recalling absolutely everything that happened while you were away. Two, feeling better than you've felt in years. Three, becoming aware of where you are and the situation in the room. Four, feeling wonderful, and five, eyes opening and feeling great!

You will be amazed at the stories you hear. The variety of places people visit never ceases to amaze me. Some will have traveled to a place as far away as it is possible to go and remain on Earth. Some will have traveled around and explored strange fantasy worlds. Others might have stayed inside the room. A few may have started, but then become nervous and instantly returned.

Some will have found that they started by going to the place they wanted to visit, but then went on a seemingly random trip to a variety of other places. Almost everyone will say how much they enjoyed the experience. Just occasionally, someone will report an unhappy experience. Usually, everyone will want to do it again.

Tell them that they can. All they need do is relax, open up the third eye, allow their astral double to emerge, and then travel. The element of fear is removed after people have experienced their first astral travel. Consequently, most people find it easy to repeat the experience for themselves in their own home.

You can help many people by showing them how to astral travel. It is not a subject you should push down people's throats, but when the situation seems right and the opportunity arises, you will enjoy helping other people to experience the freedom that you enjoy.

Chapter Thirteen

Experiments in Remote Viewing

IN MANY WAYS, THE TERM "REMOTE VIEWING" SOUNDS the same as astral travel. The person's consciousness visits a certain place, and then is able to report back on the experience. However, this is not the same as a true astral travel. In remote viewing the person stays in his or her body and remains fully conscious throughout.

Remote viewing is the subject of serious scientific scrutiny at present, but is in fact a very old practice. As far back as 1888, Dr. Alfred Backman in Sweden was conducting tests on hypnotic subjects. His results varied from person to person, but one experiment was particularly noteworthy.

Dr. Backman hypnotized a young girl named Alma and asked her to mentally visit the home of the Director-

General of Pilotage in Stockholm and see if he was home. Alma, still in hypnosis, reported that he was at that very moment sitting at a table in his study. She described what was on the table, including a bunch of keys. Dr. Backman asked her to shake the keys and place her hand on his shoulder to see if she could attract his attention. Alma did this three times and was convinced that she had caught his attention.

The Director-General, who had no idea that he was going to be the subject of any experiment, confirmed what had happened. He had been working at the table and suddenly noticed the bunch of keys. He wondered who had put them there. While pondering this, he caught a glimpse of a woman who he assumed was a maidservant. The second time he saw her out of the corner of his eye, he called out to her and got up to see what she was doing. However, there was no one there and, on checking further, the Director-General found that no one else had been in the room at the time.[1]

Admittedly, this is not a true example of remote viewing, because Alma was hypnotized at the time of the experiment. However, I have included this story because it shows that scientific interest in the subject goes back more than 100 years.

Betty Shine, the famous English healer and psychic, began remote viewing as a child. She was evacuated from London during the war and was lonely and homesick. She found that she could close her eyes and visit her mother to see what she was doing. In time, she was able to visit her friends and favorite places. Years later, when living in Spain, she and her daughter would practice remote viewing by letting their minds travel to nearby bars and cafés to see if any of their friends were there.[2]

Experiments like this provide excellent practice and the results are easy to evaluate. In time, you will be able to do them very quickly. If you are going to visit a certain place, sit down quietly before you leave, close your eyes, and let your mind travel there before you. See what is happening and who is there. When you arrive, you will instantly know how successful you were.

Do not be concerned if your results are mixed. You may find that you get three or four amazing hits in a row, and then have poor results for the next few. As you know, even the professionals are not correct all of the time. There may be a reason for the failures. Perhaps you were rushed and spent too little time on the exercise. Maybe you were concerned about someone or something. You may have been overtired. Simply take any failures in stride. It is a good idea to keep a record of all your attempts so that you can gauge your results after three or four months, rather than just a day or two. It is also bolstering to the ego to go through your records and see the number of successes you achieved.

Remote viewing can be very practical. Some years ago my family was trying to decide where to take our summer vacation. I mentally visited the different places we had thought about and selected the one that seemed to offer everything we wanted. We had a fabulous ten days away, and I experienced *déjà vu* feelings every time we went to places I had previously visited by remote viewing.

Betty Shine uses remote viewing in her healing work and has saved lives with it. One day, she mentally visited

182 • Astral Travel for Beginners

a patient of hers who lived hundreds of miles away. On entering the house, she saw the lady at the bottom of a flight of stairs looking very unwell. Betty phoned the lady's daughter and told her what she had seen. She called Betty back to say that her mother had fallen down the stairs and was now in the hospital. If Betty had not seen the lady by remote viewing she probably would have died.[3]

Remote viewing works independently of time and space. Joseph McMoneagle has been involved with remote viewing experiments for almost twenty years and now owns his own company, Intuitive Intelligence Applications. On one occasion he was given a specific location, a date, and a time. He was able to describe the person, the car and the setting accurately, but after a few minutes announced, "Something has changed. I think this person is dead." When he was asked what made him think that, Joseph told them that the person was now floating horizontally and was drifting into a "black void." This test was 100 percent successful, because Joseph had been asked to remote view a person who had been killed in a car accident. The time he had been given was three minutes before the crash.[4]

How does remote viewing work? Interestingly enough, scientists are coming to accept what psychics have known for thousands of years. Psychics believe that we can tap into the Akashic records, which is a collection of all experience and phenomena that have occurred since time began. With remote viewing it is possible that we tap into this source and, consequently, can find the answers that we are seeking. The Akashic records are independent of time and location. Scientists are hypothesizing about a matrix called "Virtual Reality" from which all answers are possible. Doesn't this sound exactly like the Akashic records?

Scientific interest in remote viewing has been encouraged by the military because it can provide vital, detailed information about the enemy's intentions. The Defense Intelligence Agency has employed psychics under the Stargate program to research this. Unfortunately, the popular press sensationalized what was intended as serious trials, and any future experiments will have to be conducted secretly, at least until the results can be demonstrated.

It is interesting to note that psychics do not always make the best remote viewers. This is because their psychic impressions can get in the way. Consequently, the best remote viewers, at least for military purposes, are people who are well-disciplined and can obey orders. They are specially picked and trained. It takes about a year before one of these people can achieve good results on a regular basis.

Of course, there are many other uses for remote viewing. Space scientists, for instance, can find out more about the conditions and potentials of manned flight to different planets. It would be possible to determine ahead of time what the head of a certain country intended to do. This would be extremely useful anyway, but imagine the potential of this when looking at unstable governments around the world. Long-range weather forecasting would be much easier. Someone could remote view two or three years ahead and see what the weather conditions were like. The business uses are unlimited. If someone was looking for a new idea they could remote view into the future and see what products were being used that are not available now.

I believe that we will be hearing much more about this particular use of remote viewing in the next few years as the military in different countries start using it more and more.

If you have a friend who is interested in experimenting with remote viewing, you can replicate some of the early tests that scientists conducted into this subject.

One person will start driving in his or her car. He or she will not choose a location to visit until after leaving the other person. This is to prevent the other person from inadvertently picking up the friend's thoughts telepathically. The person in the car will drive around and stop at the location at a certain, prearranged time. He or she will look around this place, but will not specifically concentrate on sending thoughts back to the other person. Although the person who stayed behind is acting as a receiver, in a sense, the person at the site is not trying to be a sender. This would change the test from remote viewing to telepathy.

At the agreed time, the person who has stayed behind relaxes completely. A progressive relaxation is a good idea. After doing this, he or she focuses on mentally locating the first person and determining where he or she may be. These impressions are written down for later verification. This person may choose to draw pictures or diagrams to illustrate the place where the other person is. Rather than writing impressions down, he or she may dictate any thoughts and feelings onto a cassette recorder.

When the other person returns you will be able to see how close the impressions were to the actuality. Take turns in each role, and keep records so that you can monitor your progress.

When you first start, you may deliberately limit the range of options. In this case, the person would drive to one of, say, six locations, and the person who is remote viewing would have to determine which one was visited. Later, when you have gained experience and expertise, you can widen the options until, ultimately, they can be limitless.

With the original experiments at SRI, the chosen places were always in the San Francisco Bay area. When it became too expensive to continually widen the target area, they began using map coordinates, which meant that any location in the world could be used. Later tests involved photographs taken from different places. One would be chosen at random, and the person who was being tested would try to describe the physical characteristics of that location.

Do not experiment too long at any one session. Keep them light-hearted and fun. Interestingly enough, your results will be better when you approach tests of this sort with a sense of playfulness. Keep records of every test, and prepare to be amazed as your percentage of successful hits improves.

Chapter Fourteen

Numerology and Astral Travel

I HAVE NEVER SEEN ANYTHING IN PRINT ON THE relationship between numerology and astral travel, and indeed, discovered it quite accidentally. In one of my psychic development classes we had spent a few weeks studying numerology before moving on to experiment with astral travel. One of my students reported that she found it easier to astral travel on certain Personal Days than on other days. Another student said that she had discovered the same thing.

Consequently, as a class, we kept records to see if everyone experienced similar results. With the first class, the results were almost identical for everyone. However, in later classes a number of differences emerged. I put the identical results of the first class down to the fact that two people had told the others the results they had experienced, and the others naturally looked to duplicate them.

However, a number of interesting similarities occurred. It appeared to be easier for most people to astral travel on some days, and much more difficult on others.

To explain this properly, I will need to cover some very basic numerology. Numerology is the study of cycles. We lead our lives in nine-year cycles, and we can also track cycles for individual months and days. In India, I have even seen numerologists giving people advice on certain hours, and although I am sure it can be done, I feel that this is taking the subject too far, as the vibrations would be extremely weak.

In numerology, we work out our Personal Year number by adding the month and day of our birth to the current year, and reducing the answer down to a single digit. Here is an example:

Charlotte was born on March 12. In 1998, she will be in a 6 Personal Year:

3	(Month)
12	(Day)
1998	(Year, using 1998 as an example)
2013	$2 + 0 + 1 + 3 = 6$

Here is another example. Philip was born on April 28.

4	(Month)
28	(Day)
1998	(Year)
2030	$2 + 0 + 3 + 0 = 5$

Philip is in a 5 Personal Year in 1998. The Personal Years move in nine-year cycles. This means that he will be in a 6 year in 1999, a 7 year in 2000, an 8 year in 2001, a 9 year in 2002, and start the cycle off again with a 1 year in 2003.

Personal Year

Each Personal Year has a meaning.

1 Personal Year. This is a year of new starts, as a whole nine-year cycle of experience is just beginning. The person will be full of enthusiasm, energy, zest for life, and will be wanting to start something. It is a year of new starts.

2 Personal Year. This is a year of patient waiting. Because it is difficult to wait and remain patient at the same time, this can be an emotionally draining year for some people. It is a time to consolidate the expansive beginnings of the 1 year and bring them back to more manageable proportions.

3 Personal Year. This is a fun year. Although the person will probably have to work hard this year, most emphasis will be placed on light-hearted, carefree activities. It is a wonderful year to make new friends, spend time with old ones, take up new hobbies and interests, and entertain and be entertained.

4 Personal Year. This is a year of hard work. The person may feel hemmed in, restricted, and limited. However, this can be a good year if the person makes plans and works steadily towards achieving them.

5 Personal Year. This is a year of change and variety. It is a good time to change anything. Some of these changes can be deliberate, but others can be totally unexpected. It is a good year for travel and for taking up unusual interests.

6 Personal Year. This is a year of home and family responsibilities. Other people—family, in a wide sense of the word—will need help, advice and a shoulder to lean on. All home and family matters are favored, making this a good year for both marriage and divorce. It is also good for buying or renovating a home, and for having children.

7 Personal Year. This is a quieter year. The person will need time by him or herself to think about things and to make plans. It is a year of quiet pleasures and serious learning. It is a good year to carry on one's education. It is also a good time to explore spiritual or metaphysical interests.

8 Personal Year. This is a money year, with all financial activities favored. Consequently, it is a good time to make investments, ask for a raise, or to buy and sell anything. An 8 Year is always a time of hard work, so the person needs to allow time to rest and relax.

9 Personal Year. This is the ending year of the cycle of experience. It is usually a pleasant year, but with some melancholy moments. This is because part of the person will be looking back and letting go of things that have outworn their use. It is never easy to let go, and we are all inclined to hang on to things long after their natural time is over.

However, during this year we are also looking ahead and making plans. There are likely to be a number of false leads, but by the end of the year the person will have a clear idea of what he or she wants to do in the next cycle, and will start on it in the 1 Personal Year.

Personal Month

The personal month is determined by adding the person's Personal Year number to the current month and reducing the result down to a single digit.

Charlotte will be in a 7 Personal Year in 1999. In January, she will be in an 8 Personal Month (7 [Personal Year] + 1 [January] = 8). February will be a 9 Personal Month for her (7 + 2 = 9), March will be a 1 Personal Month (7 + 3 = 10, and 1 + 0 = 1), and so on. Naturally, as there are 9 Personal Months and 12 calendar months, there is a duplication of three numbers every year. The Personal Months that occur in January, February and March reoccur in October, November and December. Consequently, in December Charlotte will be experiencing her second 1 Personal Month in that year (7 [Personal Year] + 1 + 2 [Month of the year] = 10, and 1 + 0 = 1).

The meanings for each Personal Month are the same as for the Personal Years, but have less power and influence. This is because the tone of the Personal Year number overrules the lesser numbers (Personal Months and Days), and also because the effect of the number lasts for just one month, rather than an entire year.

Personal Day

The Personal Day is found by adding the day of the month to the person's Personal Month number.

In January 1998, Charlotte will be in an 8 Personal Month. Consequently, on January 1 she will be in a 9 Personal Day (8 [Personal Month] + 1 [Day of the Month] = 9).

Likewise, on January 24 she will be in a 5 Personal Day. (8 [Personal Month] + 2 + 4 [Day of the Month] = 14, and 1 + 4 = 5).

Personal Days and Astral Travel

The first psychic class with which I investigated this combination found that two Personal Days were much better than the others for leaving the body. These were the 5 and 7 Personal Days.

It was easy to understand this. After all, 5 represents freedom, which could mean freedom from the physical body, and 7 represents spirituality.

However, although later classes also picked those days, they added the 3 and 9 days as well. Three represents self-expression and having fun. Nine represents endings. This was harder to understand. Perhaps the astral body represented the part of the person that was looking ahead, while the physical body looked back.

My students found it harder to astral travel on 2, 4, and 6 days. I found the 2 day hard to understand at first, as two represents intuition. However, it also indicates close relationships and patient waiting. Maybe on 2

Personal Days we are meant to pay attention to our partner rather than go off astral traveling.

Four represents limitations and restrictions. It is easy to understand how this Personal Day could hold people back.

Six represents home and family responsibilities. This probably indicates that our time and energies are better served by helping people who are close to us rather than astral traveling.

The other days (1 and 8) were considered neither good nor bad.

My experiments in this have been limited to my own students, but apart from the first group, every class has reported similar results.

Test this for yourself and see if it applies in your case. If you are experiencing difficulty in astral traveling, try the different experiments on your 3, 5, 7, and 9 Personal Days. You may have been unwittingly hampering yourself by experimenting on the more difficult Personal Days.

Chapter Fifteen

Conclusion

BY NOW YOU SHOULD HAVE A MUCH CLEARER IDEA OF what astral travel is all about. If you have not yet experienced an astral travel of your own, go back and start with mind travel. Once you can do that successfully, move on to Chapter Six and experiment with the method described there. After that, regardless of how successful you were, continue trying the different methods in Chapters Nine, Ten, and Eleven. This is because you may find a method that is easier and more enjoyable for you. I personally enjoy experimenting with different methods, and you may well find that you enjoy the variety, too. However, you may find one method that suits your needs and decide to stay with that. There are no hard and fast rules.

You will find as a side-benefit of your work in astral travel that you will become much more psychic. Many people have told me how much more intuitive and aware they became after learning how to astral travel.

You will also suffer much less stress, and the quality of your life will improve. This is because you will be able to relax and let yourself go any time you wish. This is an extremely useful skill in this fast-moving world, and can add years to your life.

You will lose all fear of death, as you will know that death is simply the ultimate astral travel that moves you on to a whole new world of experience.

You will also grow enormously—spiritually, psychically, and mentally. As a direct result of this growth, your relations with everyone you meet will become more harmonious, and you will become more successful as a result.

None of these things will happen overnight, but I can promise you that they will happen. Be patient. Don't try to *force* yourself out of your body. Relax and *allow* it to happen, and you will be astonished at the progress you make in the astral worlds.

Appendix

Chakra Meditation

THE ANCIENT SANSKRIT WRITERS CALLED THE SEVEN energy centers along the spine *chakras*, a word that means wheel or lotus.[1] The chakras are normally relaxed, fairly dormant, and full of latent energy. However, when they are stimulated in the form of a chakra meditation their rays of energy turn upwards.

Meditation also awakens *kundalini*, also known as "serpent fire." Kundalini is a dynamic spiritual force that comes from the Root Chakra. Kundalini is frequently represented by a coiled serpent, inside the Root Chakra, ready to act at any time. The snake has been considered a sexual symbol for thousands of years and consequently kundalini stimulates the sex organs, producing sperm and ova.[2] A small part of it also moves up the body, stimulating creativity in the brain. In Chakra Meditation this energy can spiral up through the different chakras to the pineal gland in the brain, providing a moment of transcendent illumination. It takes considerable practice to achieve this state, but it is worth persevering until you have it mastered. In time, this ability will enhance your intuitive perceptions, healing abilities, and spiritual understandings and loosen your hold on your physical body, allowing you to astral travel much more easily.

The Meditation

1. Lie down or sit upright. You need to be comfortable, with your spine as straight as possible. Consequently, lying flat on the floor is better than a bed, and a formal dining-room chair is better than a recliner.

2. Breathe slowly and steadily through the nose. I find it helpful to breathe in to the count of four, hold the breath for another four, and then exhale to a count of six. After a couple of minutes I exhale to the count of eight.

3. Concentrate on the base of your spine. Visualize the Root Chakra as a swirling circle of red energy. Once this is clearly in your mind, sense a yellow square inside the red circle. Inside the yellow square is a blue triangle. This is the home of the serpent. If your visualization skills are good, you may want to visualize this serpent coiled three and a half times inside the triangle.

Become aware of the incredible power of this energy center. You may feel the warmth and energy it provides reach out to encompass every part of your body.

4. Concentrate now on the Sacral Chakra, which is just an inch or so below the navel. Visualize it as a swirling ball of orange. Inside this orange color is a pale blue crescent, lying on its back to create a container. As you breathe in, visualize this container being filled with a clear, healing liquid. As you exhale, feel this healing liquid spreading throughout your body, providing you with limitless energy.

5. By now you should be feeling totally relaxed, and should be able to focus entirely on the bottom two chakras. While still focusing on these, allow yourself to also think about the Solar Chakra in your solar plexus. Visualize this as a revolving circle of yellow energy. Inside this circle is a smaller red circle, containing a triangle of a deeper red. Feel the redness intensifying as you breathe in, and softening as you exhale. Visualize the redness in the triangle burning away all signs of disease throughout your entire body.

6. Visualize the Heart Chakra as a revolving circle of green energy. Inside the green are two interlocking triangles made of beautiful gold. One triangle points up to heaven and the other points down to the Earth. Visualize the area where these two triangles overlap and feel the Sun's gentle, healing rays coming from this area to balance and harmonize your entire body.

As you breathe in and out while focusing on this chakra, feel yourself becoming lighter as your body fills with universal love.

7. Concentrate on the area of your Throat Chakra, visualizing it as a ball of perfect blue. Inside this swirling circle of blue is a red triangle containing a circle of violet energy. As you inhale, feel the violet circle filling up with creative inspiration. As you slowly exhale, allow this creativity to flow throughout your body. You will feel a sense of knowing that you can achieve anything you set your mind on.

8. Focus now on the Brow Chakra, in the middle of your forehead, slightly above and behind your eyebrows. See this as a wheel of indigo. Once you can successfully visualize this, as well as remaining aware of the previous chakras, picture a circle of gold in the middle of the indigo. The gold circle contains a petal or handle on each side. As you inhale you will notice the gold intensifying on the right side. As you exhale, see the left side increasing in luminosity.

After a few breaths, visualize a red triangle in the middle of the golden circle. Take a few more breaths and then see an eye inside the triangle. Although it is just a single eye, it conveys a wealth of love and understanding. This, of course, is the famous "third eye" and controls the pineal gland.

9. Concentrate on the area just above the crown of your head. This is the area of the Crown Chakra. Visualize a rapidly revolving circle of violet energy immediately above your head. Inside this circle is a

brilliant white light that moves outward, creating circles made up of tiny triangles. These are often known as the thousand-petalled lotus.3

10. If you have reached this far you will feel a steady stream of energy flowing the length of your spine every time you inhale. This creates an immensely powerful battery of will. You will feel a sense of power, knowledge, spiritual understanding, and love. You will also feel weightless and have a vibrant sense of well-being in every cell of your body. Ultimately, you will reach a state of pure consciousness.

11. If you are using this exercise to leave your body, pause for some minutes. When you feel the time is right, take a deep breath and hold it for as long as you can. Exhale as quickly as you can and tell yourself "Now!" You will immediately find yourself floating directly above your physical body.

If you are doing this exercise for meditation and spiritual purposes, pause for some minutes and become aware that each chakra is balanced and sending positive energy to every part of your body. Then retrace your steps one at a time, making sure that the energies of each chakra are allowed to return before moving on to the next one.

When you are finished, lie quietly for a few minutes before opening your eyes. Stretch and think about the meditation before getting up. You will feel better than you've felt in ages because you will have totally relaxed yourself, balanced and energized your chakras, and experienced a growth in love and spirituality.

It is extremely unlikely that you will be able to complete this meditation the first few times, or even the first few dozen times, you try it. This is because it is extremely difficult to focus on one chakra while continuing to remain aware of the previous ones.

The whole process is much easier if you have a teacher to guide you step by step as you start to awaken the kundalini force. In fact, it is believed that someone who has successfully completed this meditation can pass the knowledge on to another through a process known as *Shaktipat*. This information is imparted by touch, telepathy, sacred chants, or by eye fixation techniques.[4]

Notes

Introduction

1. Robert Crookall, *The Study and Practice of Astral Projection* (London: The Aquarian Press, 1961) 145.
2. The Acts of the Apostles, VIII, 39–40, The Holy Bible. All quotations from the Bible are from the King James version.
3. II Corinthians, XII, 2–4, The Holy Bible.
4. Richard Webster, *Omens, Oghams and Oracles* (St. Paul: Llewellyn Publications, 1995), 174.
5. Edmund Gurney, F. W. H. Myers, and Frank Podmore, *Phantasms of the Living* (London: Society for Psychical Research, 1886), Case 12.
6. Celia Green, *Out-of-the-Body Experiences* (London: Hamish Hamilton Limited, 1968).

204 • Notes

7. D. Scott Rogo, *Leaving the Body: A Complete Guide to Astral Projection* (Englewood Cliffs: Prentice-Hall, Inc., 1983), 5.

8. J. H. Brennan, *The Astral Projection Workbook* (Wellingborough: The Aquarian Press, 1989) 33.

9. Rogo, *Leaving the Body: A Complete Guide to Astral Projection*, 8.

10. Jenny Randles and Peter Hough, *The Afterlife: An Investigation into the Mysteries of Life and Death* (London: Judy Piatkus Publishers Limited, 1993), 207.

11. Brad Steiger, Astral Projection (West Chester: Para Research, 1982), 228.

12. Emmanuel Swedenborg, *Heaven and Hell*, translated by George F. Dole (New York: Swedenborg Foundation, Inc., 1976). For further information on Emmanuel Swedenborg, see Richard Webster, *Spirit Guides & Angel Guardians* (St. Paul: Llewellyn Publications, 1998).

13. Susy Smith, *Out-of-Body Experiences for the Millions* (Los Angeles: Sherbourne Press, Inc., 1968), 19.

14. Sylvia Fraser, *The Quest for the Fourth Monkey* (Toronto: Key Porter Books Limited, 1992), 259.

Chapter One

1. Sylvan Muldoon and Hereward Carrington, *The Projection of the Astral Body* (London: Rider and Company Limited, 1929), 19. From the Introduction by Hereward Carrington.

2. Ian Wilson, *The After Death Experience* (London: Sidgwick and Jackson, 1987), 108.

Chapter Two

1. Hereward Carrington, *Your Psychic Powers and How to Develop Them* (n.d. Reprinted Wellingborough: The Aquarian Press, 1976), 230.

2. F. W. H. Myers, *Human Personality and Survival of Bodily Death*, Volume 2 (London: Longmans Green and Company, 1903), 252.

3. Smith, *Out-of-Body Experiences for the Millions*, 70.

4. Robert Crookall, *Out-of-the-Body Experiences* (Secaucas: Citadel Press, 1970), 149.

5. Ibid, 151.

6. *Journal of the Society for Psychical Research*, Volume XIII (London: 1918), 368.

7. *Light Magazine*, Volume IV (London: 1935), 209.

8. Oliver Fox, *Astral Projection* (London: Rider and Company, n.d. Reprinted New York: University Books, Inc., 1962), 56–61.

9. Rogo, *Leaving the Body: A Complete Guide to Astral Projection*, 174–175.

10. Rodney Davies, *Discover Your Psychic Powers* (London: The Aquarian Press, 1992), 135. Originally published as *The ESP Workbook* (1987).

Chapter Three

1. Crookall, *Out-of-the-Body Experiences*, 55.

2. Sylvan Muldoon and Hereward Carrington, *The Phenomena of Astral Projection* (London: Rider and Company Limited, 1951), 200–201.

3. Carol Zaleski, *Otherworld Journeys: Accounts of Near-Death Experiences in Medieval and Modern Times* (New York: Oxford University Press, 1987).

4. George Gallup, Jr. and William Proctor, *Adventures in Immortality* (New York: McGraw-Hill Book Company, 1982), 32–41.

5. Stewart Robb, *Strange Prophecies That Came True* (New York: Ace Books, Inc., 1967), 114–117.

6. Melvin Morse, M.D., with Paul Perry, *Closer to the Light* (New York: Villard Books, 1990), 12.

7. Dr. Raymond Moody has written three books on the subject: *Life after Life* (New York: Bantam Books, 1975); *Reflections on Life After Life* (New York: Bantam Books, 1977); and *The Light Beyond* (New York: Bantam Books, 1988).

8. *St. Louis Medical and Surgical Journal* (St. Louis: February 1890).

9. C. G. Jung, *Memories, Dreams, Reflections* (London: William Collins, Sons and Company Limited and Routledge and Kegan Paul, 1963), 270–273.

10. Ibid, 275.

11. Morse, *Closer to the Light*, 18–19.

12. D. Scott Rogo, "Experiments with Blue Harary" in *Mind Beyond the Body*, D. Scott Rogo, ed. (New York: Penguin Books, 1978), 192.

13. Gurney, Myers, and Podmore, *Phantasms of the Living*, Case 146.

14. Jean Ritchie, *Inside the Supernatural* (London: HarperCollins Publishers, 1992), 95–96.

15. Ibid, 96.

16. Gavin and Yvonne Frost, *Astral Travel* (London: Granada Publishing Limited, 1982), 41.

17. Fox, *Astral Projection*, 34–35.

18. Robert A. *Monroe, Journeys out of the Body* (New York: Doubleday and Company, Inc., 1971), 208.

19. Ouspensky, P. D., *A New Model of the Universe* (n.d. Reprinted New York: Random House, and London: Routledge and Kegan Paul Limited, 1960). This is probably the most accessible of Ouspensky's works and includes a fascinating chapter titled "The Study of Dreams and Hypnotism."
20. Frederick Van Eeden, *A Study of Dreams in Proceedings of the Society for Psychical Research* Volume 26 (London: 1913), 431–461.
21. Joe H. Slate, Ph.D., *Psychic Empowerment* (St. Paul: Llewellyn Publications, 1995), 159.

Chapter Five

1. Henry Cornelius Agrippa of Nettesheim, *Three Books of Occult Philosophy*, translated by James Freake, edited and annotated by Donald Tyson (St. Paul: Llewellyn Publications, 1993), 629.
2. Fox, *Astral Projection*, 45–46.
3. Harvey Day, *Occult Illustrated Dictionary* (London: Kaye and Ward Limited, 1975), 21.
4. Brad Steiger, *ESP: Your Sixth Sense* (New York: Award Books, 1966), 103–106.
5. Nandor Fodor, *Encyclopaedia of Psychic Science* (New York: University Books, Inc., 1966), 103 and J. H. Brennan, *The Astral Projection Workbook* (Wellingborough: The Aquarian Press, 1989), 11.
6. Fodor, *Encyclopaedia of Psychic Science*, 100.
7. *Census of Hallucinations, Proceedings of the Society for Psychical Research*, Volume 12 (London: Society for Psychical Research, 1894).
8. Steiger, *Astral Projection*, 92.
9. Fodor, *Encyclopaedia of Psychic Science*, 232.
10. Steiger, *ESP: Your Sixth Sense*, 106–107.

Chapter Six

1. Yram, *Practical Astral Projection* (n.d. Reprinted New York: Samuel Weiser, Inc., 1967), 64.

2. There is a story that is similar to this in Cornelius Agrippa's *Three Books of Occult Philosophy*, 631. Hermotinus of Clazomenae frequently astral traveled to different countries and was away from his body for several days at a time. His wife treacherously told Hermotinus' enemies about these astral travels, and they came and burned his body while he was away. Consequently, his soul was never able to return to its body. This makes a good story, but is, in fact, impossible. At the first sign of any potential danger to the physical body, the astral double is instantly returned so that the person can handle the situation.

Chapter Seven

1. Charles T. Tart, "A Psychophysiological Study of Out-of-the-Body Experiences in a Selected Subject" in *Mind Beyond the Body*, D. Scott Rogo, ed. (New York: Penguin Books, 1978), 103–128. Originally published in *Journal of the American Society for Psychical Research*, Volume 62 (1968), 3–27.

2. Charles Panati, *Quadrangle/The Supersenses: Our Potential for Parasensory Experience* (New York: New York Times Book Company, 1974), 145.

3. Eileen Garrett's words quoted in Dr. Douglas M. Baker, *Practical Techniques of Astral Projection* (Wellingborough: The Aquarian Press, 1977), 22.

4. Green, *Out-of-the-Body Experiences*.

5. Yram, *Practical Astral Projection*, 62 and 66, and Sylvan Muldoon and Hereward Carrington, *Projection of the Astral Body* (London: Rider and Company, 1929), 13.

6. Lyall Watson, *The Romeo Error* (London: Hodder and Stoughton Limited, 1974), 143.

7. Ecclesiastes, XII, 6, The Holy Bible.

8. Muldoon and Carrington, *The Projection of the Astral Body*, 59–60.

9. Hilary Evans, *Visions, Apparitions, Alien Visitors* (Wellingborough: The Aquarian Press, 1984), 203–204.

10. Rogo, ed., *Mind Beyond the Body*, 20–21.

11. Rogo, *Leaving the Body: A Complete Guide to Astral Projection*, 176.

12. Yram, *Practical Astral Projection*, 70–71.

13. Muldoon and Carrington, *The Projection of the Astral Body*, 58.

14. Frost and Frost, *Astral Travel*, 59.

15. In *The Projection of the Astral Body*, 53, Sylvan Muldoon described his return from his first out-of-body experience as "every muscle of the physical jerked, and a penetrating pain, as if I had been split open from head to foot, shot through me."

Chapter Eight

1. Yram, *Practical Astral Projection*, 61–62.

2. Monroe, *Journeys Out of the Body*, 128.

3. Ibid, 131.

4. Yram, *Practical Astral Projection*, 99.

5. Ibid, 137.

6. Fox, *Astral Projection*, 32–33.

7. Migene González-Wippler, *The Complete Book of Spells, Ceremonies, and Magic* (New York: Crown Publishers, Inc., 1978), 97.

8. Geoffrey of Monmouth, *The History of the Kings of Britain*, translated by Lewis Thorpe (London: The Folio Society, 1969), 145.

9. D. J. Conway, *Astral Love* (St. Paul: Llewellyn Publications, 1996), 39.

Chapter Nine

1. Fox, *Astral Projection*, 126–132. Oliver Fox called this method "Way of Self-Induced Trance."

2. Rogo, *Leaving the Body: A Complete Guide to Astral Projection*, 20.

3. Hector Durville, "Experimental Researches Concerning Phantoms of the Living" in *Annals of Psychical Science*, Volume 7 (1908), 335–344.

4. Prescott Hall, "Digest of Spirit Teachings Received through Mrs. Minnie E. Keeler" in *Journal of the American Society for Psychical Research*, Volume 10 (1916), 632–660 and 679–708.

5. Robert Crookall, *The Techniques of Astral Projection* (London: The Aquarian Press, 1964), XX.

6. *Journal of the American Society for Psychical Research*, Volume 10 (1916), 706.

7. Ibid, 681.

8. Ibid, 643.

9. Ibid, 708.

10. Ibid, 649.

11. Prescott Hall, "Experiments in Astral Projection" in *Journal of the American Society for Psychical Research*, Volume 12 (1918), 39–60.

12. Yram, *Practical Astral Projection*, 60.

13. For more information on the chakras see Richard Webster, *Aura Reading for Beginners* (St. Paul: Llewellyn Publications, 1998); Bill Whitcomb, *The Magician's Companion* (St. Paul: Llewellyn Publications, 1993); and Peter Rendel, *Introduction to the Chakras* (Wellingborough: The Aquarian Press, 1974).

14. Ritchie, *Inside the Supernatural*, 161–164.

15. G. M. Glaskin, *Windows of the Mind* (London: Wildwood House Limited, 1974); *Worlds Within* (London: Wildwood House, 1976); and *A Door to Infinity: Proving the Christos Experience* (New York: Avery Publishing Group, 1979).

16. Two articles on the subject are J. Palmer and R. Oieberman, "ESP and Out-of-Body Experiences: A Further Study," and "ESP and Out-of-Body Experiences: The Effect of Psychological Set" in J. D. Morris, W. G. Roll, and R. L. Morris, eds., *Research in Parapsychology* (Metuchen: Scarecrow Press, 1975), 122–127.

17. Mrs. Henry Sidgwick, "On the Evidence for Clairvoyance" in *Proceedings of the Society for Psychical Research*, Volume VII (1891).

Chapter Thirteen

1. Dr. Alfred Backman, "Experiments in Clairvoyance" in *Proceedings of the Society for Psychical Research*, Volume 7, Part 19 (1891).

2. Betty Shine, *Mind Waves* (London: Bantam Press, 1993), 103–104.

3. Ibid, 110–111.

4. Jerry Snider, interview with Joseph McMoneagle in *Magical Blend*, Issue #52.

Appendix

1. Webster, *Aura Reading for Beginners*, 1998.

2. Dr. Jonn Mumford, *A Chakra and Kundalini Workbook*, 2nd edition (St. Paul: Llewellyn Publications, 1994), 73.

3. Each chakra vibrates at a different frequency and this is indicated by the number of petals used to represent it. The Root Chakra has just four petals, indicating the low vibrations of the material world. The Crown Chakra, represented by 1,000 petals, symbolizes its high vibrational rate and potential in the transcendent worlds.

4. Charles Breaux, *Journey into Consciousness* (New York: Nicolas-Hays, Inc., 1989), 15.

Glossary

Akashic Records—The Akashic records are a collection or storehouse that contains all the knowledge of humankind from the beginning to the end of time. They are believed to be located in an area of the astral plane known as astral light.

Astral—The term *astral* comes from a Greek word meaning "related to a star." It originally described the location of the abodes of the Greek gods.

Astral Body—The astral body is a duplicate of the physical body that is constructed of much finer vibrations. It is used as a vehicle to travel through the astral planes.

Astral Double—Another name for **Astral Body.**

Astral Light—Astral light is the area on the astral plane where the Akashic records are kept. It gains its name from the high energy vibrations created by the melding of the past, present, and future.

Astral Plane—The astral plane is a parallel world that reflects our physical world, but operates on a higher vibrational level. The astral plane consists of seven subplanes:

1. The Astral Cemetery, where the astral body disintegrates when the soul leaves the astral plane to reincarnate or move on to a higher plane.

2 The Astral Shell, which is the temporary home of the astral body after the soul has left and before it drops to the Astral cemetery.

3. The Astral Hell, which is the home of the most debased and debauched human souls.

4. Sleeping Regions, where souls rest for some time after their physical death and become prepared for their new position in the astral plane.

5. The Intellectual Plane, which is the home of the astral bodies who were not able to complete a creative or intellectual project while they were in the physical world. When the soul reincarnates it is able to bring this work to completion in the physical world.

6. The Heroic Plane, not surprisingly, houses the heroes who are able to reenact and relive their greatest victories.

7. The Mystical Plane, which is home to the mystics and religious leaders of every faith.

Astral Projection—Astral projection is the ability to project or remove the astral body from the physical body and use it to travel on the astral plane.

Astral Travel—The ability to move about the astral plane in the astral body, while the physical body remains behind.

Autoscopy—See **Doppelganger.**

Bilocation—Bilocation is the ability to be in two different places at the same time. The physical body is in one location while the astral body is making itself visible in another.

Chakras—The chakras (pronounced Kah-krahs) are seven energy centers located in the human energy field between the base of the spine and the top of the head. The word *chakra* is a Sanskrit word that means "wheel," which is appropriate as they are normally seen as whirling circles of energy. The word also means a "blossoming flower," which is why chakras are often depicted as lotus flowers.

Déjà vu—Déjà vu literally means "already seen." It is the experience of perceiving a new situation as if it had occurred before.

Doppelganger—A doppelganger is a human double and occurs when the physical body unexpectedly meets the astral body. The correct name for this phenomenon is autoscopy.

Entity—An entity is a being who lives in the astral plane. Consequently, it possesses an astral body but has no physical body.

Etheric Double—Another name for **Astral Body.**

Hypnogogic State—A hypnogogic state is the drowsy, hypnotic-like state that is present immediately before falling asleep.

Kundalini—Kundalini is the energy stream that lies latent in the Root Chakra. Using Kundalini Yoga (originally known as Laya Yoga) or meditation techniques, this energy can be used to energize all of the chakras. Kundalini is often depicted as a serpent coiled three and a half times around an upright lingam.

Lucid Dreaming—A lucid dream is a dream that the person is able to control and direct. The person is aware that he or she is dreaming but does not wake up. The term was coined by Dr. Frederick Van Eeden in 1913.

Near-Death Experience (NDE)—A near-death experience occurs when someone feels that death is about to occur, and experiences a situation in which the consciousness appears to be separated from the physical body.

Out-of-Body Experience (OBE)—An out-of-body experience is what one experiences when the astral body leaves the physical body and travels on the astral plane.

Parapsychologist—A parapsychologist is a scientist who specializes in the study of psychic phenomena.

Psychic Protection—Psychic protection consists of a series of activities, or a ritual, performed before engaging in any psychic work. It is designed to protect the person from any form of outside attack.

Rapid Eye Movements (REM)—Rapid eye movements occur in clusters of five to sixty minutes' duration, several times a night, while one is asleep. They occur when the person is dreaming. To test this idea, sleepers were awakened and questioned during or immediately following an REM period. People awakened at this time could recall their dreams in great detail. When they were awakened at other times they either could not recall any dreams, or else saw them as vague, brief thoughts.

Remote Viewing—Remote viewing is a term devised by the research scientists at SRI International in 1972 to describe experiments in which people were able to psychically sense what was happening at certain places far from the location of the experiment.

Silver Cord—A cord or line of energy that connects the physical and astral bodies while the person is astral traveling.

Teleportation—Teleportation is the sudden transportation of a person or object from one place to another.

Suggested Reading

Baker, Dr. Douglas M. *Practical Techniques of Astral Projection*. Wellingborough: The Aquarian Press, 1977.

Barrett, Sir William. *Death-Bed Visions*. 1926. Reprint, Wellingborough: The Aquarian Press, 1986.

Barton, Winifred G. *Meditation and Astral Projection*. Ottawa: Psi Science Productions, 1974.

Brennan, J. H. *Astral Doorways*. New York: Samuel Weiser, Inc., 1971.

Brennan, J. H. *The Astral Projection Workbook*. Wellingborough: The Aquarian Press, 1989; New York: Sterling Publishing Co. Inc.,1990.

Conway, D. J. *Flying Without a Broom*. St. Paul, MN: Llewellyn Publications, 1995.

Crookall, Robert. *The Study and Practice of Astral Projection*. London: The Aquarian Press, 1961.

———. *The Techniques of Astral Travel*. London: The Aquarian Press, 1964.

———. *More Astral Projections: Analyses of Case Histories*. London: The Aquarian Press, 1964.

———. *The Mechanisms of Astral Projection*. Moradabad: Darshana International, 1969.

———. *Out-Of-The-Body Experiences*. Secaucus: The Citadel Press, 1970.

Denning, Melita and Osborne Phillips. *Astral Projection: The Out-of-Body Experience*. St. Paul: Llewellyn Publications, 1990.

Fox, Oliver. *Astral Projection*. n.d. (c. 1939). Reprint, New Hyde Park: University Books, 1962.

Glaskin, G. M. *Windows of the Mind: The Christos Experience*. London: Wildwood House Limited, 1974.

———. *Worlds Within: Probing the Christos Experience*. London: Wildwood House Limited, 1976.

———. *A Door to Infinity: Proving the Christos Experience*. New York: Avery Publishing Group, 1979.

Green, Celia. *Out-Of-The-Body Experiences*. Oxford: Institute for Psychophysical Research, 1968.

Frost, Gavin and Yvonne. *Astral Travel*. London: Granada Publishing Limited, 1982.

Harary, Keith and Russell Targ. *Mind Race*. New York: Villard Books, 1984.

Leadbeater, Charles. *The Astral Plane*. Wheaton: Theosophical Publishing House, 1933.

McMoneagle, Joseph. *Mind Trek*. Norfolk: Hampton Roads Press, 1993.

Monroe, Robert A. *Journeys out of the Body*. New York: Doubleday and Company, Inc., 1971.

———. *Far Journeys*. New York: Doubleday and Company, Inc., 1985.

———. *Ultimate Journey*. New York: Doubleday and Company, Inc., 1994.

Moser, Robert E. *Mental and Astral Projection*. Cottonwood: Esoteric Publications, 1974.

Muldoon, Sylvan and Hereward Carrington. *The Projection of the Astral Body*. London: Rider and Company Limited, 1929.

———. *The Case for Astral Projection*. Chicago: Aries Press, 1936.

———. *The Phenomena of Astral Projection*. London: Rider and Company, 1951.

Rogo, Scott D, ed. *Mind Beyond the Body: The Mystery of ESP Projection*. New York: Penguin Books, 1978.

Rogo, D. Scott. *Leaving the Body*. Englewood Cliffs: Prentice-Hall, Inc., 1983.

Shine, Betty. *Mind Waves*. London: Bantam Press, 1993.

Smith, Susy. *Out-Of-Body Experiences for the Millions*. New York: Sherbourne Press, Inc., 1968.

Steiger, Brad. *Astral Projection*. West Chester: Para Research, 1982.

Yram, Practical *Astral Projection*. n.d. Reprint, New York: Samuel Weiser, Inc., 1967.

Zaleski, Carol. *Otherworld Journeys*. New York: Oxford University Press, Inc., 1987.

Index

A

Affirmation method, 124

Agrippa, Cornelius, 58

Akashic records, 182–183

Alcohol, 7–8, 67, 111, 172

American Society for
Psychical Research, 82,
108–109

Anthony, St., 63

Astral body, xv, 1, 4–7, 13–15,
19, 21, 25–26, 37, 67, 69,
83–86, 90–91, 105–109,
117, 120, 172, 175

Astral plane, 4–5, 17, 59, 80,
91, 94–95, 98–99

Astral sex, 98–99

Astral travel, 3–6, 8–11,
13–14, 16–21, 24, 39,
41–42, 46, 55, 58–59, 61,
63, 79–80, 90–93, 97, 99,
101, 103–105, 107–111,
113–115, 117–119, 121,
123, 125, 127, 129, 131,
133, 135, 137–139, 141,
143, 145, 147, 163, 165,
193

Autoscopy, 65

B

Ba, xi

Backman, Dr. Alfred, 179–180

Beard, S. H., xvii

Bernard, Dr. Eugene E., xvii
Bible, xii, 85, 203, 209
Bilocation, 61–63, 65, 215
Biofeedback, 9
Blavatsky, Madame, xiv
Brougham, Lord, 35–36
Brow chakra, 122, 200
Brunton, Paul, 15
Bulford, Staveley, 15

C

Callaway, Hugh, xiv
Carrington, Hereward, xiv,
    13, 110
Cayce, Edgar, xix
Chakra method, 121, 124
Chakras, 121–124, 197–202
Christos experience, 126
City of Limerick, 64
Clark, Kim, 32–33
Consciousness, 1, 5, 14,
    20–21, 25, 33, 40–41, 67,
    75, 102–103, 112, 117,
    119, 121–122, 124, 147,
    160, 162, 176, 179, 201
Costa, Guiseppe, 25
Coué, Emil, 124
Crisis visions, 34–36
Crookall, Dr. Robert, xv,
    xvi, 15, 85, 110, 203,
    205, 210
Crowley, Aleister, 118
Crown chakra, 122, 124, 200

D

Defense Intelligence
    Agency, 183
Deja vu, 46, 181, 215
Deprivation, 33, 72
Doppelgangers, 65–67
Dougal, Dr. Serena Roney,
    122
Dream of Knowledge, 39
Dreams, xiii, 21, 24, 37–43,
    45, 217
Drugs, 7–8, 33, 67, 102,
    111, 172
Durville, Hector, xiii, 106

E

Egypt, xi, xii, 15, 24
Entities, 5, 59, 96, 98
Etheric double, 13, 106

F

Fear, x, 2–3, 5, 30, 80, 83,
    97, 172, 178, 196
Forham, Marcel Louis, xiv
Fox, Oliver, xiv, 17–18,
    39–40, 58–59, 97, 101
French method, 105

G

G, Riley, 88
Gallup Poll, 24
Galvanic skin response, 9
Garrett, Eileen, 84, 208
Geoffrey of Monmouth, 98

Gerhardi, William, 16
Glabella, 14
Glaskin, G. M., 126–127
Goethe, Johann Wolfgang
von, 66
Green, Celia, xvi, 85, 89,
203
Guides, 96, 129–130, 136,
150–152, 155–156, 163,
177, 202
Gurney, Edmund, xvii, 35,
203

H

Hallucinogen, 102, 122
Haraldson, Erlendur, 36
Harary, Keith, 19, 33, 39,
81, 89
Heart chakra, 122, 199
Helpers, 96
Hemingway, Ernest, xix
Hitchcock, P. J., 23
Hout, Dr. R. B., 16–17
Hutchinson Island, 88
Hypnogogic stage, 38
Hypnotism, 62, 130, 132
Hypnotism method, 130
Hyslop, Professor James,
109

I

India, xi, 31, 35, 188
Issels, Dr. Josef, 9

J

Jung, Carl, 30–31, 206

K

Ka, xi, xii
Keeler, Minnie, 108–111
Kundalini, 197, 202, 216

L

Lancelin, Dr Charles,
106–108
Landau, Eileen, 87
Landau, Lucian, 87
Laubscher, B. J. F., 85
Liguori, Alphonse de, 61
Limoges, 63
Lucid dreaming, 40, 42

M

MacDonald, William, 62
McKenzie, James Hewat, 67
McMoneagle, Joseph, 182
Meditation, 102, 104, 121,
124, 166, 197–202
Meditation method, 102,
104
Merlin, 98
Mind travel, 46–47, 53, 55,
71, 75, 104, 181, 195
Monroe, Robert, 40, 96–97
Moody, Dr. Raymond A.,
28–29
Morris, Dr. Robert, 19
Morse, Dr. Melvin, 32–33

Muldoon, Sylvan, x, xiv, xv, 8, 39, 41, 72, 78, 85, 91, 110

N

Near–death experience, 25–26, 30–33
Numerology, 187–189, 191, 193

O

Osis, Dr. Karlis, 82
Ouspensky, P. D., 40

P

Payne, Phoebe, 24
Perez, Gil, 68–69
Personal Day, 192–193
Personal Month, 191–192
Personal Year, 188–191
Pineal gland, 122, 198, 200
Podolsky, Dr. Edward, 66
Progressive relaxation, 39, 47, 50, 54, 75, 83, 102, 104–105, 126, 130–132, 136–137, 151–152, 184
Psychic energy, 79, 121
Psychic protection, 73
Psychical Research Foundation, 19

R

Rapid eye movements, 37
Remote viewing, xvii, 20–21, 179–185
Rhine, Dr. Louisa, 36
Rig veda, 6
Ringberg Clinic, 9
Ritchie, George, 28
Rogo, D. Scott, 19
Root chakra, 122, 124, 197–198
Rushmore, Mount, 88–89

S

Sacral chakra, 122, 124, 199
Sanskrit, 121, 197
Schlansker, Nellie, 24
Serpent fire, 197
Shaktipat, 202
Shine, Betty, 180, 182
Silver cord, xx, 14–17, 84–85, 95, 160
Slate, Dr. Joe H., 43
Society for Psychical Research, 63, 82, 87, 108–109, 132
Solar chakra, 122, 199
Stanford Research Institute, 20
Stargate, 183
Stead, William T., 90
Swann, Ingo, 81–83
Swedenborg, Emmanuel, xviii, xix
Swing method, 104

T

Tait, Richard, 64–65
Tart, Dr Charles, 82
Teleportation, 68
Temple of Poseidon, 46
Theosophical Society, xiv
Third eye, 127, 159, 162,
    174–175, 178, 200
Throat chakra, 122, 200
Tibet, xi
Toloachi, 98
Turney, Vincent, 15
Twemlow, Dr. Stewart, xvi

V

Van Eeden, Dr Frederick,
    42
Virtual reality, 183
Visualization method,
    118–119
Visualization, 54, 114–118,
    198

W

Wein, Professor, 62
Weserman, Herr, xiii
Whirlwind method, 108
Willpower method,
    119–120, 133
Wilmot case, 63
Wiltse, Dr A. S., 15, 29

Y

Yram, xiv, 72–73, 85, 90,
    96, 108, 113–114

Z

Zaleski, Carol, 24

Aura Reading
for Beginners

*Develop Your Psychic
Awareness for Health
& Success*

Richard Webster

When you lose your temper, don't be surprised if a dirty red haze suddenly appears around you. If you do something magnanimous, your aura will expand. Now you can learn to see the energy that emanates off yourself and other people through the proven methods taught by Richard Webster in his psychic training classes.

Learn to feel the aura, see the colors in it, and interpret what those colors mean. Explore the chakra system, and how to restore balance to chakras that are over- or under-stimulated. Then you can begin to imprint your desires into your aura to attract what you want in your life.

These proven methods for seeing the aura will help you:

- Interpret the meanings of colors in the aura
- Find a career that is best suited for you
- Relate better to people you meet and deal with
- Discover areas of your life that you need to work on
- Discover the signs of impending ill health
- Change the state of your aura and stimulate specific chakras through music, crystals, color

1-56718-798-6, 5³⁄₁₆ x 8, 208 pp., illus. $9.95

To order, call 1–800 THE MOON
Prices subject to change without notice